Shergar

A True Crime Story of Kidnapping, Racehorse and Politics

Conrad Bauer

Copyrights

Disclaimer and Terms of Use

ISBN: 9781795443821

Printed in the United States

MAPLEWOOD
— PUBLISHING —

Contents

Introduction

Ask anyone in Great Britain or Ireland about famous racehorses, and they'll likely have only one name to tell you: Shergar. At his peak, Shergar was one of the most elegant, powerful, and successful racehorses in the history of the sport. By the time he retired, his reputation alone was enough to earn huge amounts of money. But then, one cold night, he vanished. Kidnapped. Stolen by a group of masked men. The heist quickly became an international sensation, attracting attention from around the world. Everyone wanted to know.

Who kidnapped Shergar?

And the mystery has continued to the present day. Still a cold case, picking apart the Gordian knot of Shergar's disappearance involves everything from bad business deals to domestic terrorism. The Irish Republican Army has been accused of being at the center of the plot, arriving as it did amid the Troubles in the country. Occurring during one of the most turbulent times in the history of Ireland, the kidnapping of one of the nation's sporting heroes was not only front-page news, it was intrinsically linked to the political situation in the country. As the kidnappers issued their demands and the owners tried desperately to get their horse back, the situation sank deeper and deeper into tragedy before the trail went cold.

In this book, we will look into the complicated and fascinating disappearance of Shergar. We will examine the delicate domestic situation in Ireland and probe just how this battle with the British might have spilled over

1

into the sport of kings. We will look at the people who became embroiled in the plot on every side, and we will try to uncover the truth behind one of the world's strangest kidnapping cases. By the end of this book, we just might know what happened to the horse named Shergar.

8th February, 1983 - A Kidnapping

The sun had already set over the yard. It was a February night in County Kildare, which meant the evening drew in quick behind a thick blanket of clouds. There was no rain that night, and by 20:30 that evening, there was still a little bit of light lingering over the stables. As might be expected out in the countryside, the sounds were almost entirely natural. Owls, wind, even the occasional fox. Every now and then there was a burst of breath from one of the horses housed in the buildings. These were not normal horses. Now securely shut up behind lock and key, these were racehorses. What's more, they were winning racehorses. Their calling out in the night was not the same, natural sounds that echoed around the Irish countryside. They were pampered, cared for, and indulged. These were champions, horses who had proved themselves against the rest of the world. Now living in semi-retirement, their duty was simply to procreate, to bring forth more race-winning horses into the world. Along with the clang and clatter of usual yard work, the horses would whisper and bluster, clapping their hooves against the ground. Tonight, however, they were silent.

County Kildare by day

The stable yard was dead. The biting cold had taken its toll, forcing the horses into an early night and driving the grooms into their homes. Once all the horses had been put into their stalls, James Fitzgerald had been more than happy to close the door behind him. His house was located near the stables, conveniently close to the horses should any need arise. Tasked with caring for some of the very best horses in Irish racing history, he took his job very seriously. With the incredible value attached to these creatures, the owners were pleased to have found someone who could provide the very best care. By this time in the night, James had gone into the home he shared with his family. Thinking himself done, James entered his home, greeted his family, and began to relax. There might be a need to go back into the yard at some point, but with the cold and the dark the way it was, he hoped that his work was done.

As James began to settle into his evening, he did not hear the Ford Granada pulling into the yard. The tires rolled slowly over the concrete, dragging a heavy horse trailer behind. The lights were dimmed in the yard, everyone apparently having gone to bed. The car and trailer crawled to a halt in front of the stables. The car doors opened. Out stepped a gang of men.

Back inside the groom's home, James twitched. He had a nagging sensation that he had heard something in the yard, but it seemed that it had stopped. It might just have been a trick of the night. It might have been a car. If it was, then there would be a knock shortly. But the noise seemed to have stopped. James forgot about the sound, turning back to his family and their evening at hand.

At 20:40, there was a sharp knock at the door. James's son, Bernard Fitzgerald, ran to answer it. As he pulled open the door, the cold of the night rushed into the hallway, drawing up and around a tall figure wearing a policeman's uniform. The man was dressed head to toe as one of the Irish Garda, including a thick balaclava placed over his face. It was an understandable concession to the cruel February temperatures. Before Bernard could ask anything, there was a grumbling voice from behind the black fabric.

"Is he in?"

Bernard instantly assumed it would be a call for his father. It might be something to do with the horses. Or his car, maybe? It could have been the police bringing bad news. The thoughts rushed through Bernard's head as he turned from the door and began to move back down the hallway. He didn't get far. As the boy turned, the figure in black whipped out an arm and struck him across the small of his back. The blow knocked the boy to the floor with a bang. It was enough to rouse James from his seat, and the groom came running into the hall.

When James entered, he saw his son lying face down, clutching at his back. The Garda was above him, looming in through the doorway. There was a shout halfway up James' throat when it caught. Suddenly, his eyes had been drawn to the little pistol held in the Garda's hand. It was a short weapon, snub-nosed but intimidating. More importantly, it was pointing directly at James. The implication was clear. As the pistol kept the Fitzgerald family in check, three more figures pushed in the hallway. The last of them was also armed, carrying with him a submachine gun. It all seemed like too heavy an arsenal to rob a stable groom.

As the men marched into the house, it appeared to James that they were incredibly calm. The groom himself could feel the blood rushing through his veins, could feel his heart pounding and the adrenaline rushing through his body. Despite the weapons, the priority for James was his family. They must be kept safe. As the guns were pointed, the men calmly filed into the home and gathered together the Fitzgerald family.

There was a clear organization. The group seemed to know exactly what they were doing and were clearly accustomed to the presence of guns. The same could not be said for the Fitzgerald family. James watched as the men maneuvered his wife and children into a tight group. As they did so, they referred to one another only as "Cresswell." It was clearly a code name, the same for each of them. When the men were satisfied that they had gathered the entire family together, one of them motioned towards James. The groom was told to collect his coat. As he dressed for the evening air, two of the intruders escorted him outside.

They marched together through the night. The silence and the calmness of the air betrayed the brutality of the evening. Even in spite of all the upheaval and the fear that had occurred, James Fitzgerald found himself walking a familiar path. He led the two men through the stable block, out of the yard, and into the area where the studs were kept.

This was the most important part of the stables. Here, the owners housed some of their most precious horses, those who possessed the means to create a dynasty of racing legends. With a bit of foresight, a bit of planning, a bit of breeding skill, and a bit of luck, these stallions could father the next Grand National winner five times over. And the pick of the bunch was a horse James knew all too well. Shergar. The horse was worth millions, even in the 1980s. He had won races around Britain, finally retiring and being encouraged to sire a generation of equally as competitive horses. James was Shergar's groom, and he knew the horse better than almost anyone. James was the one who cleaned his stable, polished his hooves, and spoke to the horse every single day. Shergar was almost one of the family. James was leading the men right to the horse's stall.

Once they arrived, the horse seemed to be happy. Often, animals can sense fear and intimidation in people, perhaps smelling the emotion in the air. But James stayed calm. The guns were hidden from view now. Out of sight, out of mind. Slowly, he reached into the stall and patted the horse. It was still early in the evening, though dark enough. James knew what he had to do.

The masked men directed him as he led the horse out of the stall, through the yard, and along the path they'd just walked. Shergar came quietly, flanks of heavy muscle moving softly beneath the bay skin. With a start, the horse could have bolted and run. They would never have been able to catch him, especially in the night. Shergar was a champion horse. But he came quietly.

When the three men and the horse arrived back in the yard, the men encouraged James to load the horse up into the trailer. With his eyes now used to the dark, James could pick out the figures moving. As well as the men in the house, it seemed as though there were six of them in all. Six men, with at least two guns. They had his family. They were going to take his horse. James complied, doing exactly what he was told.

Once the horse was loaded and secured, James stepped back. The car began to pull away slowly, pulling the horse trailer behind it. James watched as Shergar was towed unwittingly into the night. These men were thieves. They had come for the horse. While he might not have been able to save Shergar, James still hoped to save his family. And himself. The repercussions would have to wait until tomorrow. There was going to be a huge amount of anger. You cannot just steal a racehorse, James thought.

But before he could dwell too long on what was happening, James found himself being bundled into a car. Still with a pistol pointing at his person, James was driven away from his family. The men drove in silence, getting further and further away from the stables and the house. They continued to drive him around for three hours. It was tense. In the early hours of the morning, the car pulled over. One of the men dragged James close and whispered in his ear. This, he was told, is the password. Don't forget it. And with that, James Fitzgerald was thrown from the car.

Left alone in the night, James stood up. He was glad for the coat the robbers had made him wear, but now he was alone. There was no telling what had happened back at the Fitzgerald family home. There was no way to know where the horse had been taken. There was not even an indication as to who the men might be, or as to why they might want to steal Shergar. James Fitzgerald found himself cold and alone in the early hours of the morning. There was no choice in the matter now. He would just have to walk home. In the bitter chill of the February morning, the countryside of County Kildare seemed almost calm. As James walked, attempting to find his way home, this silent stroll through the night would be his last period of calm for a long, long time. By the time the sun rose, James Fitzgerald would find himself at the center of one of the strangest, most complicated, and potentially most dangerous kidnapping cases in the history of Ireland. Shergar was gone, and nobody knew where.

A United Ireland

Why all this fuss for a horse? The kidnapping that took place on the 8th of February, 1983, was a national sensation. Horses, to the majority of the public, were far from a major concern. Even watching the annual Grand National race on British television might show one or two horses that fell during the race, after which the vets and the officials erect a curtain around the fallen creature and put it out of its misery. After one broken leg, these races horses could never fulfil their ambitions. Their lives were cut short. If the loss of a horse was a regular threat in the world of racing, then what should it matter if one horse went missing in the night? Put simply, Shergar was far more than just a horse. And to complicate matters, Ireland of the 1980s was far more than a normal country.

Nicknamed "Ireland's Pegasus," Shergar was a national hero. However, he had the bad luck of being born at a time when Ireland's nationhood was a matter of fierce debate. The "Troubles," the battle for control of Northern Ireland, was one of the most dangerous and difficult times in the history of Great Britain and Ireland. Occasionally, however, great moments could allow for such difficulties to be overlooked. In 1978, when a colt was born with four white socks and what would become a trademark flash across his face, few could have predicted that this young horse would become such a figure. In time, this foal would become one of Ireland's most famous residents, for the right reasons and for the wrong reasons. As well as the records he set on the racetrack that made him famous, the story of Shergar's disappearance would make him infamous.

Skipping over the majority of the history between Great Britain and Ireland, it is safe to say that the relationship between the two countries has always been fractious. Following Irish independence and the formation of the Republic of Ireland in the early Twentieth Century, it seemed as though the countries might be going some way to repairing their differences. But there was one sticking point. Though the majority of the island of Ireland was now part of the Republic, a large swath of land in the northeastern corner remained under British rule. Known as Northern Ireland, the Troubles emerged between those who felt that the land should be returned to the Republic and those who felt it should remain as a part of Great Britain.

This fight involved two very distinct ideas of national identity. There were also religious issues, swept along in the political wake, that soon made one's personal beliefs an article of war. Though nominally not a religious conflict, there was a clear separation between the Protestant side of the country and the Catholic side. The former was allied closely to the loyalists and the British, while the latter found themselves siding with the Republicans. The war was at first concerned with nationality and then with religion. Evolving into a sectarian conflict, the Troubles were a complicated mess of ideals, beliefs, and traditions, fought fiercely on both sides.

The goals of both sides were quite simple to establish. The republicans in Northern Ireland (those who were almost exclusively catholic) wanted Northern Ireland to be united with the Republic of Ireland to the south. This would have ended British rule on the island, something that had been in place for centuries. On the other side of the fence, the loyalists (the majority of whom were Protestant) wanted to continue to keep a constitutional link to the British monarchy. Both sides felt passionate about their beliefs. Both sides rose up in arms. Both the republicans and the loyalists soon found themselves amassing a paramilitary force. Both were prepared to use violence. Only one of them, it seemed, could emerge victorious.

Belfast during the troubles

The Troubles in Northern Ireland are usually considered as having occurred between 1968, when a series of civil rights protests took place, and 1998, when the Good Friday Agreement was signed. Between these two periods, there were bursts of intense violence that sometimes extended beyond Northern Ireland itself. For a thirty-year period, people in the Republic of Ireland, Northern Ireland, and Great Britain lived under the shadow of the Troubles. Many people died, many were hurt, and many people lost loved ones. It was an incredibly difficult time for every country involved, and it should not have been a surprise to see that those living under these conditions were able to fall so quickly for a sporting hero. The success of sporting heroes such as Shergar provided an element of escapism, a chance to get away from the difficulties of the ongoing conflict. Eventually, however, this too would become deeply entwined with the Troubles.

This brings us to the story at hand. While many books, academic papers, and documentaries dealing with the history and the importance of the Troubles have been created, we will only be able to pay the war a passing glance. It is the backdrop against which this kidnapping tale takes place. Now that we have covered the two sides of the conflict, it is time to introduce the group that will become one of the key players: The Irish Republican Army, otherwise known as the IRA.

During the conflicts, a number of groups emerged on both sides. Few became a famous (or as notorious) as the IRA. Things are complicated by the fact that the actual IRA split into two separate factions as early as 1969. On one side, there were the "Officials" who were based in Dublin. This group hoped to find a peaceful solution to the conflict, seeking a socialist union of the two countries under one Republic rule. On the other side were the "Provisionals," who were based in Belfast and had taken a vow to separate themselves from British rule by any means necessary, including the use of violence. This made things complicated, as both groups continued to make use of the IRA moniker, rejecting the legitimate existence of the other side.

Still from Provisional IRA propaganda video

The Officials have gone on to become a legitimate political party, transitioning to the group known as Sinn Fein, which means Ourselves Alone in the Irish language. These days, they hold a number of parliamentary seats in both the Republic of Ireland and Northern Ireland. When the latter MPs come to vote, they abstain from visiting Westminster in London, refusing to accept the legitimacy of British governance over Northern Ireland. These days, after the majority of British troops have been removed from Northern Ireland and loyalist forces such as the Royal Ulster Constabulary have been long since disbanded, the Officials' form of peaceful opposition has become the key battleground for Republican concerns.

For the Provisionals, however, the approach to securing unification was much more violent. Making use of tactics such as direct military opposition to British troops, guerrilla warfare in Belfast, and bombings on the British mainland, they waged a bloody and fierce war to secure independence. Their efforts were met equally by the loyalists, with both sides giving as good as they got in terms of violence and bloodshed. The Provisional IRA would most often be blamed for many of the most destructive deeds in Northern Ireland. They were strongly criticized in the British press and became the figureheads of the Irish resistance in every respect. With regards to this story, it is the Provisional IRA who were heavily implicated. As they fought against the British in 1983, the Troubles were still very much alive. This is the context into which we must step; having some understanding of the conflict in Northern Ireland at the time. This is necessary to fathom exactly why a group might seek to kidnap a racehorse, what they might stand to gain, and why the crime might eventually go unsolved.

As well as the Provisional IRA, we will also take time to stop in with Middle Eastern Princes, gangs of masked criminals, bungled police operations, secret groups, frenzied press, and a baffled public. All of these arrived in Ireland in 1983, and all concerned themselves with the horse that had vanished into the thick fog of a cold Irish night.

The stables themselves could be found in County Kildare. Named the Curragh after the Irish word for racecourse (spelled Cuirreach), the site was composed of some 5,000 acres of countryside. The lands were vast, reflecting their importance to Irish horseracing culture. The stables are still not only a private concern, but are also home to the Irish National Stud. There are training facilities and caring facilities of the highest quality available. Nowhere in Ireland are horses better cared for.

Part of the reason for this is the ground itself, with the soil containing a large percentage of sand, which makes for excellent drainage and a perfect surface for horses. The Curragh can trace itself back to the Eighteenth Century, when the first race was held on the grounds. The first derby was there in 1866, and the site has even been recognized by the Irish parliament for its quality and importance.

But there is also a hidden history to Curragh. At various times during its history, the grounds have been used as a training base for the Irish Army. It has been used to intern prisoners, often those of a military persuasion.

At the time of the kidnapping, the Curragh was most famous as a racetrack and a stables. There are five main races held at the facility every year, the biggest races in Ireland. The course is famously right-handed, and appropriately enough, bends around in a horseshoe shape over a two-mile stretch. Due to the importance of Irish racing on a global scale, the eyes of the horse racing world are attracted to Curragh on a regular basis, and the name itself is well-known within the sport.

There are also the stud facilities. For anyone interested in horse racing, the pedigree of a runner is always important. When a racing dynasty is established, the ability to breed and train horses becomes big money. When these horses win, their breeding potential is measured in the millions. If, for example, a champion stallion is put to stud when his racing career is over, the owner can earn a huge amount just from selling his offspring. With the ancestry of racehorses taken very seriously, the breeding is a key element of this. At the Curragh, the stud facilities are excellent.

Perhaps the most famous of all the stud facilities at the Curragh is the Ballymany Stud. The entrance to this block is placed right beside the course, just at the point where training usually kicks into a gallop. Ballymany was the stables when Shergar lived, where he was put out to stud at the time of his disappearance. Most interestingly of all, in 1983, they belonged to a man titled the Aga Khan IV. The Aga Khan was not only a British Citizen, but he was considered the spiritual leader of the Ismaili Muslims, a group which totaled some 15 million. Aga Khan was a title that had been passed down in the family, and the Aga Khan IV's personal worth was estimated at just under a billion dollars. The Aga Khan was the owner and operator of the Ballymany Stud Facilities, having taken an interest in racehorses of the highest quality. It was a grand operation, demonstrated by the very arrival of Shergar to the facility. When the horse first arrived at Ballymany, his presence was celebrated with a parade and a pipe band. By this point, he was already a national hero. Adored by the Irish public, Shergar was set to spend his retirement fathering the next generation of champion horses at one of the best stud facilities in the world.

The Aga Khan IV had inherited the stud facility from his grandfather, the Aga Khan III. The elder Khan had been introduced to the European version of the sport by Colonel Hall-Walker in 1904. The Englishman had shown the young Indian prince not only the sport itself, but also the stable he owned in County Kildare. The Colonel's introductions paved the way for the prince to enter into the world of racing, which he did so with relish. In possession of a large fortune, the Aga Khan III was very much of the opinion that he would do everything to the very highest standard. This meant investing heavily in the breeding facilities, hiring the very best people in the business, and ensuring that his horses were the very best. This paid off by the 1920s, when the he began to see the successes pile up. Winning many major racing honors, he was soon very highly regarded within racing circles as a man who knew the sport well. After he died in 1957, a complicated line of succession eventually led to the Aga Khan IV Prince Shah Karim Al Hussaini taking over. By this time, he was ingrained enough in the British society that Queen Elizabeth II would refer to the Aga Khan as his Highness, despite the young man being aged just twenty.

Aga Khan (left) in 1959

The Aga Khan IV found that he had inherited a vastly successful racing empire, along with his religious importance and personal fortunes. The horses he now owned continued to win and win well. After his first season in the sport, he managed to walk away with over 1.1 million francs in prize money from France alone. Though the majority of the family's racing interests were in France, the Aga Khan began to race more and more in England over the coming decades. By the 1980s, his roster of horses had doubled in size. Many of these were based in England, and in 1978, a pair of trainers named Michael Stoute and Fulke Johnson-Houghton took in a group of yearlings (horses that are one year old) and started to train them. Even from those early days, one horse stood out from the rest. With four white feet and a distinctive flash across his face, the horse would rise to fame as Shergar. At this time, however, he was just another yearling under the control of the Aga Khan, being trained by Michael Stoute.

Stoute himself plays an important role in this story. Nowadays known as Sir Michael Stoute, his position within the horseracing community is assured. In part, that is thanks to his work with Shergar. Born in 1945 in Barbados, he left the Caribbean at the age of 19 and became an assistant to Pat Rohan, a famous English horse trainer. By 1972, he was training his own horses, and his list of winners was growing longer and increasingly prestigious. During the course of his career, he has been awarded the title of Champion Trainer as many as ten times, with his list of winning races including everything from the King George VI to the Dubai World Cup. Shergar holds an important place in Stoute's career, as he was the first horse to win the Epsom Derby under Stoute's tutelage. Since then, Stoute has had winners in 1986, 2003, and 2004. Winning a knighthood for his services to Barbados and its tourism industry, Stoute was famously the trainer of Estimate, the winner of the Gold Cup in 2013. Estimate's owner was none other than Queen Elizabeth II of England. As you can see, there were few men more deeply ingrained in the horseracing community and few men who had more of the community's undoubting respect.

In addition to Stoute, it is important to introduce Walter Swinburn. Nicknamed "the Choirboy," Walter Swinburn was a jockey and a very good one at that. Born in Oxford, he rode his first winner at the age of just 17. Coming from strong horseracing stock, the entire Swinburn family loved the sport. This involvement led to Walter being trained at the Frenchie Nicholson Jockey School, one of the best institutions in the country. It would be a pairing with Shergar that brought the Choirboy his greatest fame, as the pair won the 1981 Epsom Derby by ten lengths, a huge distance. Like Stoute, Swinburn would have later successes in the race and would win it another two times after the Shergar incident. Racing around the world, Swinburn was a jockey of international renown. These days, having retired from racing, Swinburn has been involved in training and horse ownership. Despite the difficulties that both Swinburn and Stoute would experience during the time we will examine, they have both remained heavily involved with the sport.

Alongside Swinburn and Stoute, there is one other key player in the incredible success story. Shergar himself was the most famous horse in the world. At the peak of his powers, he was known as the Pegasus of Ireland. Shergar was the youngest player in this story. Born in 1978, he was immediately recognizable for his distinctive colors. Each of his four feet were white, as though they had been dipped in paint. Similarly, there was a distinctive splash of color across Shergar's face. Otherwise, he was entirely bay, that color particular to horses that seems like a living mixture of red and brown, matte and shining all at once. One of the horse's most endearing behaviors only became apparent when he started racing, as his tongue would loll out of the side of his mouth while galloping at full tilt.

Like all racehorses, Shergar's pedigree was stringently documented. His father was a horse named "Great Nephew." Great Nephew was born in Britain but found most of his success in France, eventually winning some $180,000 in prize money. As well as Shergar, Great Nephew also fathered "Grundy" (another Derby Stakes winner), "Carotene," "Mrs. Penny," and "Tolmi." All of them were successful to some degree, leading Great Nephew to win the retirement title of Leading Sire in England on two different occasions. On the other side of the family, Shergar's mother was "Sharmeen." Also more successful in France than anywhere else, she won a number of races, though rarely managed to break through into headline-grabbing territory. Together, however, Sharmeen and Great Nephew managed to provide the world with one of the greatest racehorses of all time.

If you take a quick look at Shergar's race record, it might be hard to see why he is held in such high regard. Totaling only eight races and with results as a two year old that were far from legendary, the horse's early efforts were commendable if not stunning. However, this changed in 1980 when Shergar entered into the Kris Plate and won by two lengths in a field of 23 horses. He set a record for the course at Newbury when he was being ridden by Lester Piggott, a legendary jockey.

During that year, Shergar's only other race was the William Hill Futility Stakes (named for the bookies), a race which he lost by two and a half lengths, though he managed to finish second.

It was in Shergar's third year that he truly started to show his form. It was noted that his real strength lay in his ability to chase down and power past other horses, leaving them struggling behind him. It was a trait shared by other horses such as Secretariat and Phar Lap, both of whom are held in high regard in the sport. So in 1981, Shergar's training began to focus on making the most of his qualities. Though there was little in the exercises to hint at what was to come, both Michael Stoute and the Aga Khan were notably excited about Shergar's potential. They hoped that this potential would eventually make the most of the horse's fine breeding and they would have quite the racehorse on their hands. They would be proved right. To really understand what set Shergar apart, it helps to take his career race by race.

First up was the Guardian Classic. Taking place on the 25th of April, Walter Swinburn was in the saddle. Aged 19, he and Shergar chased down the first win in the horse's first race of the season. At the time, Walter Swinburn was a relatively unknown force. His racing pedigree was similar to that of his ride, though his grandfather in particular was known as a skilled jockey. During the race, Shergar demonstrated the abilities that would soon mark him out as one of the most exciting competitors in the sporting world. Not only did the horse and jockey pull up alongside and power past their rivals with ten furlongs still to run, but they went on to win the race by ten lengths. For those with little experience in racing, this is a very good distance, indicative of how much better the winner is when compared to his rivals. Not only that, but the other racers were no slouches. Kirtling, who came in second (and was a cousin of Shergar), would go on to win the Dee Stakes held at Chester by six lengths. The victory was so impressive that Richard Baerlein, who was covering the race for the Observer, would famously claim that the odds of 8-1 for Shergar at the Derby should prompt every one of his readers to "bet like men." It was the start of something spectacular.

The second race of the year was the Chester Vase. Traditionally, people see the Chester Vase as the best indicator of the future winner of the Epsom Derby. Manage a victory in Chester, and people will be talking about it right up to Derby day. The race took place on the 5th of May, and the ten-furlong race was a breeze for Shergar. He won by about twelve lengths, another resounding victory. Already the odds of his placing first in the Derby were being slashed. Leaving the rest of the pack behind, Shergar seemed to stroll to the win, almost as though he wasn't even racing at all. As thousands of cheering fans watched on, he seemed to breeze his way effortlessly to the first place finish. By this point, everyone in the horseracing world was waking up to Shergar.

The Chester Vase provided the run up to one of the racing calendar's biggest events, the Epsom Derby. By the day of the race, Shergar was installed as the favorite. Those who had followed Richard Baerlein's advice and placed their bets at 8-1 seemed pretty happy with their efforts. As ever, thousands of people arrived on the day of the race. A packed schedule led up to the main event, though the only name on people's lips was

Shergar. By the start of the race, he had moved from being an outsider to 11-10 on, easily the favorite. The crowds were not disappointed. Not only did Shergar win, but he did so in style. As the pack passed through Tattenham Corner, the last bend before the final straight, Shergar was third. The track is set up is a hairpin shape, with the horses coming out of Tattenham corner picking up speed as the track takes a slight slope. They hit the home stretch, which inclined just before the finish line. With Shergar in third, Walter Swinburn encouraged him to unleash his power. The pair were riding in their first Derby, but they showed no fear. With Swinburn geeing the horse on to greater and greater speeds, the pair began to steamroll their way into first place. With a nose in front, they didn't stop there. By the end of the home stretch, Shergar and Swinburn were a full ten lengths ahead. It was the biggest margin of victory ever seen in the Epsom Derby, and it immediately thrust the horse and rider into the history books. There were even some who said that Shergar could have been encouraged to drive on a little harder, perhaps winning by 15 lengths, had Swinburn felt the need to push. According to the jockey, however, the horse "found his own pace" early in the race. There wasn't much Swinburn needed to do. Shergar knew how to win. The jockey simply piloted the wonder horse to victory. So big was the distance between first and second that the rider of the second-placed horse, Glint of Gold, joked that he thought he had won the race before realizing that there was another horse way ahead on the horizon.

The win in the Epsom Derby was important for a number of reasons. It cemented Shergar's place in the pantheon of racing legends, going so far as to rank in the Observer's Most Memorable Sporting Moments of the

20th Century. It was important for the Aga Khan IV, the owner, who recorded his first Derby win as an owner. His grandfather, the man who had realized the family's position in the Western horseracing world, had won five. Despite having a long way to go, the Aga Khan IV's victory with Shergar was perhaps more memorable than any of his grandfather's wins. It was an important day for Richard Baerlein. The journalist had been an early proponent of Shergar and had been backing him consistently for weeks. As the odds dwindled from 33-1 to odds on favorite, he continued to back Shergar, making himself a decent amount of money. So much, in fact, that he was able to buy a house in Sussex, a home which he immediately named "Shergar."

But most importantly, the result was important for the racing public. According to many sources, the win felt like a once-in-a-lifetime moment. Straight away, it was heralded as one of the greatest Derby wins of all time, the first major win for both Swinburn and Shergar. For the former, it would not be his last. Later wins, however, were never as memorable as that day in 1981.

So how can you possibly follow up a win like the one in Epsom? If you're Shergar, then the next target seems obvious. Another Derby. This time, the Irish Derby. For the fourth race, there was no Walter Swinburn. Instead, Lester Piggott was in the irons. This was Shergar's homecoming after the victorious display in Epsom. The race was held in Curragh, near the stud facility where Shergar would eventually be housed. Piggott was a fine choice as the rider. A man who won nine Epsom Derbies throughout his career, he knew when to let the horse run its own race. For Shergar, this was perfect. Just as in Epsom, Shergar rounded the final corner before leaving his rivals in the dust. With his immense power, he pulled forward and away from the pack. This time, he won by four lengths. It might not have been quite so resounding, but the relaxed stride of the horse demonstrated just how comfortable a victory it really was. As the commentator on the day, Peter O'Sullevan, proclaimed, Shergar was "only in an exercise canter." Up until that point, only 13 horses had won the Epsom Derby and the Irish Derby. For Irish racing fans, a star had been born. With every win and every race, Shergar was writing his name into the history books and making himself a firm favorite with the Irish natives.

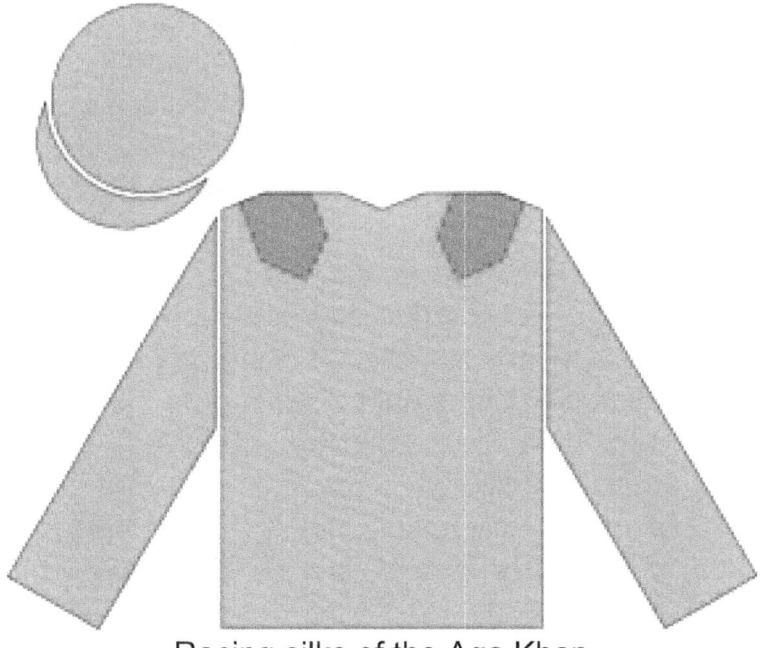

Racing silks of the Aga Khan

There were still two races to run that year. First, there was the George VI and Queen Elizabeth Stakes, otherwise known as the King George. Run every year along the famous track at Ascot, the race is a mile and four furlongs. Easily one of the most prestigious races in the world, open only to horses aged three or more, the prize money was second only at the time to the Epsom Derby. For this race, Swinburn was brought back and paired up with Shergar. As ever in racing, the colors worn by the jockey are dictated by the owner. For the Aga Khan, this was a set of green silks with orange flashes on the shoulders. Every time Shergar ran, the jockey would be wearing the colors of the Aga Khan. A quick look through photos of the races and it's easy to recognize Shergar, whoever might be riding. As well as the fifth race of the year, this would be the first time that Shergar had faced horses older than he was. It made people wonder whether the prodigious power could be replicated when placed next to older, wilier opponents. Just like before, the race was tight right up until the final straight. As soon as the ground flattened out before him, Shergar switched on the afterburners and swept past the pack. The race was won by four lengths.

After the King George, the Aga Khan found himself facing a difficult decision. With racehorses, the majority of the money is not to be made in race winnings (which are unpredictable) but in renting the horse out as a stud. With Shergar's exemplary racing record, many people would spend a great deal of money to buy one of his offspring. Accordingly, the Aga Khan split the ownership of the horse into 40 shares. Thirty-four of these were sold for £250,000 each, while he kept six shares for himself. This valued Shergar at £10 million. At the time, it was a record for a stallion at stud. Even looking through the list of people who bought a share can provide insight into the world of racing. Anyone who knew anything about racing wanted a share in the horse. Tim Rogers, Robert Sangster, John Magnier, Lord Derby, and Paddy McGrath, as well as established stud farms such as Lockridge, Bluefield, Mainland, Coolmore, and many others.

The decision to sell stakes in Shergar is essential to this story. Not only does it demonstrate that this was a horse at the absolute pinnacle of the sport, but it spreads around the interest that was held in his continued existence. When he was kidnapped, it was not just one owner who felt the sting. Instead, each shareholder witnessed their investment disappear into the night inside the mysterious horse trailer. Added to this, it shows the amount of money involved. While we might normally expect a kidnapping to involve a large ransom fee, the value of the kidnap victim itself shows just how big a crime had taken place. Just after Shergar won the King George, he was the most famous name in horse racing. In a global sport, Shergar was the aspirational hero, the leader of the pack. His value reflected this, and his fame spread to those who were only vaguely aware of the sport. In Ireland, his popularity was beyond belief. It was this success, this fame, and this value that would make him such a target. But before Shergar took off to the stud farm, there was one more race left to win.

The season was ending with the St. Leger Stakes. This was to be the final event of the racing calendar for everyone's favorite horse. By this point, the new stakeholders had invested their money and were keen to watch as their £10 million horse took to the track. It would be the last time Shergar would be able to race as a three year old, and it was planned to be a warm-up for one of the biggest races in France, the Prix de l'Arc de Triomphe. By the time the horses lined up, Shergar was a 6-4 favorite. The race unfolded in the usual manner, with Shergar staying close to the pack as they entered the straight. But this time something was different. Whereas horse and jockey would normally pull away in a phenomenal display of strength, Shergar began to flag. The horse was losing energy at a rate that shocked Swinburn, the jockey. Swinburn turned to the whip to try and encourage the horse to break into his usual victorious stride, but it was not enough. Shergar finished fourth. If you had not known that this was the famous Shergar, then he would have seemed like any other middle-of-the-pack runner.

Due to the fame and notoriety of Shergar, lips were abuzz about the performance. Everyone had a theory about what had gone wrong and about the horse's lackluster performance. Everything was suggested, from complacency to muddy ground to too long a distance to drugs. Certain people put it down as a bad day at the office, others described it as the natural end in a run of magnificent form. Others tried to concoct wild conspiracy theories that included radio-controlled steroid injection devices hidden beneath the wrapping tape on the horse's leg. It might even have been natural fatigue after one of the most extraordinary seasons in a racing career. Whatever the explanation, no one was talking about the winner of the race. Shergar was still everyone's favorite horse. However, following the race, the Aga Khan decided to remove Shergar from the French event. He hoped to leave Shergar's fantastic record untarnished by further failures. The Timeform rating, used to rank and measure the performance of racehorses, kept Shergar at 140, a total given only to the very best horses around. To the owners, it made better sense to keep this intact, to ensure Shergar's value stayed high, and to reap the bountiful profits to be made from the stud industry.

And so Shergar retired, barely three years old. Unsurprisingly, he had been named the European Horse of the Year for 1981, though he had already retired by September. Placed into the Ballymany Stud facility owned and operated by the Aga Khan, it was hoped that a new generation of champions would be sired by everyone's favorite horse. With a bit of luck, they might even be half as successful as their father. There had been rumors that he might even make the long trip to the United States of America, where some horses are put to stud for great profits. It was decided that he would remain in Ireland, however, surrounded by a country that adored him. There was precedent for this. Phar Lap raced during the Great Depression and was adored by huge numbers of the population in Australia and New Zealand, said to bring smiles to thousands of faces in difficult times. Well, times were difficult in Ireland now, and the successes of Shergar were enough to provide a momentary respite from the Troubles.

For some insight into just how profitable an enterprise horse breeding can be, we can look at the first year which Shergar spent at Ballymany. During these twelve months, he was paired with 35 mares. This would cost £80,000 each time, meaning that nearly £3 million was raised simply through one year in the stud farm. With profits like that, it's easy to see why so many people were interested in investing in the horse. The next year was set to be even bigger, with as many as 55 potential mares arranged to pair with Shergar during 1983. However, that dream would die on the 8th of February. As we know, the arrival of the armed men in the night ended a happy retirement. For Ireland's favorite racehorse, life was about to take an unpleasant turn. Shergar was about to make the move from famous to infamous.

Negotiations

We have already examined the events of the 8th of February, 1983. We saw first-hand how a gang of armed men arrived and made away with a champion racehorse in the dead of night. But the effects of the crime were felt far beyond the walls of Ballymany. The stud farm might well have been the scene of the crime, but the kidnapping itself was national and international news. In the swirling fog, as the masked men entered the groom's home and brandished their machine guns, there was little indication of the ramifications that would be felt across the world. But this was far more than a daring kidnapping. It was far more than some Hollywood blockbuster-style caper. The ramifications of that night extended far beyond Ballymany and affected the course of horse racing and Irish history. As we will soon see, the kidnapping of Shergar was a huge event.

But before we look at the wider influence of the evening in question, let's examine the events once more. Jim Fitzgerald had been a stable boy since he was just 14 years old. Aged 53 in 1983, he had perfected his craft enough to be put in charge of caring for the world's most famous racehorse, housed at Ballymany. Shergar was worth £10 million, with a long and profitable career ahead of him, so it was fitting that his caretaker would be a vastly experienced man. Furthermore, Fitzgerald lived right next to the stables, rarely out of ear shot of the horse.

At 20:40 that evening, there was a knock on his door. Bernard Fitzgerald, Jim's son opened the door to find a man dressed as a police officer. In the yard, a Ford

Granada (allegedly) could be seen towing a horse trailer. Just behind it was a van. A third car pulled into the yard. A simple latch on the gate had been the only security they had needed to bypass. It had offered no security. As Bernard turned back into the house to fetch his father, the man in the police uniform struck him on the back of the head. As the boy fell to the floor, Jim wandered into the hallway to see what the fuss was about. He was met with the business end of a pistol, while three more masked men walked into the home. Behind them, a further four criminals could be seen. The family was led into the kitchen, by which time Jim had spotted a machine gun and a rifle in addition to the pistol. The men announced that they were there to steal the horse and that they would want £2 million in exchange for his safe return.

Ten minutes after arriving, while two men were left in the kitchen to guard the family, the rest of the gang marched Jim Fitzgerald to the stables at gun point. They demanded to be led to Shergar and then demanded help in moving the racehorse into the trailer they'd brought with them. According to the stable hand, the horse would only be moved by a familiar face. Had the men tried to move Shergar themselves, they would have failed. Trying to encourage a horse into a horse trailer can be difficult at the best of times. If the horse was nervous or simply did not wish to cooperate, then it could become almost impossible. Nevertheless, Jim Fitzgerald encouraged Shergar into the trailer. It was something that he would later feel terrible about, but with a gun pointing at his family and with the prospect of seeing the horse returned alive and unharmed, it seemed like an understandable decision. According to Jim Fitzgerald, it seemed like at least one man knew how to handle a horse, and he noted that they were equipped with short wave radios.

The identities of the men would remain one of the biggest questions surrounding the case. While the majority wore masks throughout, there were a few key moments when faces were visible. Peter Cullen, a deputy head groom at the farm, was one man who gave the police evidence of some men he had seen hanging around the stable entrance. Meanwhile, Cullen's children would give the police reports some five weeks later, reports that pertained to similarities between certain individuals and figures who had been seen in or near the stables on the night in question.

After helping put Shergar into the horse trailer, Jim Fitzgerald was led back into his home. He was held there for an hour before being bundled into the back of one of the vehicles the kidnappers had brought with them. While he was made to lie face down (unable to see where he was going), the gang drove him around for close to four hours. Eventually, he was deposited outside Kilcock, just twenty miles from the farm. Later, Jim confessed to the anxiety he felt on the night. Time and time again, he was warned of the horrible violence that would not only be visited upon him, but on his family as well. Should Jim have the temerity to go to the police, the gang would return with a vengeance. Just before being thrown out at Kilcock, Jim was given a code name, "King Neptune." It was to be used by the kidnappers in their communications. Once he was booted from the vehicle, Jim made his way to a nearby Chinese restaurant. It was the early hours of the morning, but he managed to raise someone who let him inside. There, he called up his brother and asked to be picked up. At around one in the morning, Jim placed a call to Ghislain Drion – the stud manager at Ballymany – and warned him of the ramifications of calling the police. Once he had learned what had happened, Drion drove out to the farm, got in touch with Stan Cosgrove, the stud vet, and they began to plan their next move.

The first thing they had to do was to inform the owner. This meant calling the Aga Khan, who was in Switzerland at the time. It was 3 o'clock in the morning when the call was finally placed. The chief question on everyone's minds was whether or not the authorities should be alerted. The kidnappers had made it very clear that any indication of any police involvement would not be looked upon kindly. By 4 o'clock, more and more people were being drafted into the meeting. The kidnapping was important, and people were quick to respond despite the hour. Stan Cosgrove got in touch with Sean Berry, formerly a captain in the Army, who in turn placed a call to Alan Dukes. Dukes was the Irish Finance Minister at the time, and he put the racing men in touch with Michael Noonan, the Justice Minister. Dukes, not knowing how to react to the bizarre crime, later confessed that he simply passed on the number for Michael Noonan and went back to bed. Already, word of the kidnapping was spreading through the highest levels of government. By the time Shergar had been kidnapped for eight hours, two of Ireland's top politicians had been consulted, and the problem was with the Aga Khan over in Switzerland. Already, it was a matter of international importance.

With so many people involved in the kidnapping, it was going to be increasingly difficult to keep the matter private. There is no doubt that the ideal situation for the kidnappers was that the problem be resolved quickly and quietly, with the victim paying up the required sum immediately and without the police getting involved. As the word reached Irish politicians in the early hours of the morning, it was quickly becoming apparent that such a quiet operation would simply not be possible. Shergar was a national figure. Even the whisper of a rumor that something was out of the ordinary would quickly hit the headlines.

It was decided to wait to hear from the kidnappers. Over the coming days, Ghislain Drion began to conduct negotiations with the man who referred to himself as King Neptune. This was not as simple as it might have seemed, however. Drion, a Frenchman, had great difficulty in understanding the thick Irish accents of the kidnappers. They, in turn, struggled to comprehend his French inflections. Things broke down when it became apparent that the owners of the horse considered the ransom demanded to be "unreasonable and illogical." So extreme, in fact, did they consider the demands, that a few people began to question whether the kidnappers were honestly expecting to succeed. It was almost as though they were purposefully stating ridiculous demands so that the owners would have little choice but to refuse.

The Aga Khan responded. The owner decided to bring in a professional. He settled on a former member of the British armed forces to help steer the situation in the right direction. The man was a once a member of the SAS (the Special Air Service). Khan charged him with the negotiations and dealings with the kidnappers. The aim was to have Shergar returned unharmed. To everyone's dismay, the discussions between the SAS man and King Neptune also reached an impasse.

Since the tense negotiations, a huge amount of blame has been laid at the door of the kidnappers. They have been accused of bungling the dealings, of throwing away their chance at actually receiving a ransom. For a team that demonstrated such expert precision in kidnapping the horse, their attempt to negotiate with the owners were almost comically bad. One example of this was their lack of research. They believed that the Aga Khan was the sole owner of Shergar, seemingly unaware of the sales of shares in the horse that had taken place a year earlier. They did not know about the other 34 members of the syndicate that had valued the horse at £10 million. For anyone with even a passing knowledge of the racing world, this was basic information. Similarly, the ransom of £2 million was requested to be paid in £100 notes. No such note existed at the time. One of the seeming strokes of genius that had been apparent at the time of the kidnapping – the date was just before a local racehorse sale, meaning every road was packed with horse trailers, far too many to search – was beginning to look more and more like blind luck.

There was definitely a willingness on the part of the owners to negotiate with the kidnappers. Sir Jackie Astor was the man who had put the Aga Khan in touch with the SAS officer and later admitted that the owners viewed the situation as resolvable. However, they were unwilling to pay a ransom. The reasoning was clear. If the owners caved this time and delivered a fortune to the kidnappers, then every racehorse around the world was instantly a target. As noted with Shergar, many of these horses were under very lax security. Should the Aga

Khan and the rest of the owners pay up, then there was little that could be done to protect the other horses around the world. They might have considered paying a reward for information that led to the return of Shergar, but paying huge sums to the kidnappers was out of the question entirely, if only to protect the sport of horseracing as a whole. The whole situation was a mess, however, with the owners squabbling among themselves, facing financial complications and dwindling time.

For their part, the kidnappers tried to steer the negotiations in their favor. They requested that three racing journalists be brought into the negotiations to act as intermediaries. It was thought that these men would add a touch of expertise to the proceedings, as well as demonstrate the severity of the situation at hand. The journalists would know full well just what an important figure Shergar had become. The choice of journalists was important. One of the best known was Peter "Tommo" Thompson. For 25 years, he had been known as the face of racing in Ireland, with his jovial approach to coverage on the television. Alongside Thompson, the kidnappers requested John Oaksey, a racing presenter, and Peter Campling, who worked for the Sun newspaper. All three would be asked to help with the negotiations. Their involvement would become well-known, to the point where – even years later – Peter Thompson would tell tales of the conspiracy theories that people pass along to him and whisper behind his back. Occasionally, they'll even offer up a solution to the crime, claiming inside knowledge. But the rumors never spread beyond hearsay. If anything, they simply demonstrated how quickly the three journalists became the faces of the negotiations.

Their experience was not as simple as dialing up the kidnappers. As Thompson told it, all three men were taken to the Europa Hotel, an institution which held the odd claim to fame of being the most bombed hotel anywhere in Europe. At the height of the Troubles, this piece of trivia did not go unnoticed. With Belfast being one of the most dangerous cities in the world in 1983, the Europe Hotel in the center of the city seemed a pointedly chosen location for any deal to go down.

After he arrived, Thompson received a phone call. The voice on the other end of the line informed him that he was being watched. Over the next eight hours, Thompson was told to remain in the hotel. During this time, he was called a further eight times and each call lasted exactly a minute. This was thirty seconds shy of what the technicians said they would need to place a trace on the call. Once again, the kidnappers seemed to really know their business. At one point, Thompson managed to keep the voice on the line talking. He broke through the minute barrier, then for another ten seconds, then ten seconds more. As they talked, Thompson was increasingly aware that he was surely into the right territory. When the call finally finished, it was revealed that it had lasted 1 minute and 35 seconds, just over the required amount. Thompson's delight was soon scuttled, however, when the technicians revealed that the man in charge of the tracing had just finished his shift. The call had not been traced. The kidnappers did not make the same mistake again. When talking about the case years later, Thompson revealed that he believed that this incident would be one of the most crucial mistakes made during the operation.

This all came to naught the following Monday. On that day, Peter Thompson received another phone call. The voice on the other end of the line provided him with a simple message. The horse was dead. There would be no more phone calls.

The Aftermath

Once Peter Thompson received that phone call, everyone quickly realized the scale of the situation. There had been suspicions that all was not right, but the chilling bluntness of the call left few people with any doubts as to whether the horse was alive. The kidnappers had made blunders, matched in their ineptitude by those who sought to return the horse to its rightful owners. Now, neither side had achieved their goals. The kidnappers were implicated in an international scandal. The owners had lost an incredibly valuable asset. Those who had worked with Shergar had lost a beloved animal. The Irish public (and racing fans around the world) had lost one of the most adored idols in sport. Everyone, it seemed, had lost.

As such, there was an immediate clamor to point the finger of blame. If the horse could not be returned home, then it would be important to resolve the situation and bring those responsible to justice. This would prove even more difficult than anyone might ever have imagined. There were clues scattered across the story of Shergar and his kidnapping, but putting them together only seemed to create more questions than answers. The investigators were left with a riddle wrapped in an enigma. There were suspicions and rumors, though few of these could be substantiated. So what were the most compelling pieces of evidence?

We should return first to Peter Thompson. As we have seen, Thompson was not only incredibly close to the kidnapping of Shergar, but his position as a journalist meant that he had a good reading of the situation. He was able to separate fact from fiction, even if most of the information lay in the gray area between the two. As an Irishman, he knew the political situation of the country. As a sports and racing fan, he knew the importance of Shergar. As a journalist, he knew how big a story this really was. According to Thompson – discussing the matter many years later – the chief suspect in the case is the IRA. We will examine this claim in greater detail later, but it is important to look into one telling piece of evidence.

As told by Thompson, the discussions with the kidnappers were always curt and to the point. It became a habit to use a code word, in order for the two parties to confirm that they were indeed speaking to the right people. The code word was different each time but was always the name of a famous racehorse. When the name was said during the phone call, Thompson could be sure that he had the real kidnappers on the phone. These names were revealed during the course of the investigation. All of the names, bar one. Thompson kept one of the names to himself and never published it. He never told anyone. But one day, he saw it in print.

It was in a book, and that book belonged to Sean O'Callaghan. Sean had been a member of the IRA and had killed people during his time with the group, but he had switched his allegiance. During the Troubles, he had become an informer for the police and passed on detailed information about the IRA's plans. This made him a wanted man. Despite this, O'Callaghan published his story. He wrote a book, appropriately titled *The Informer*. When Peter Thompson finally got around to reading the story of the IRA insider, he was shocked to see the code name printed on the page. It was the same one he had kept to himself, the one that only the kidnappers had known. As Thompson recounted, it "shook [him] to the core."

Sean O'Callaghan's book goes into some detail about how the kidnapping was done. Though some have questioned the author's account of his time with the IRA and whether he is telling the entire truth, it remained one of the best accounts of the night of the kidnapping and the aftermath of the negotiation attempts. As told in the text, Sean O'Callaghan was part of a nine-man team. Alongside him were seven "former Provos" (Provos being the name given to members of the Provisional Irish Republican Army). Together, the group had devised the plan while serving time in prison. The chief organizers were a veteran member of the IRA and a man who had been a bookie's clerk on the outside. O'Callaghan claimed that the man at the head of the operation was none other than Kevin Mallon, the man who would become infamous for a violent prison escape in which he shot his way out from behind bars, as well as being broken out by a daring helicopter raid from another prison. Mallon was one of the most famous members of the Provos and was consistently wanted by the police, at least when he wasn't already behind bars. In addition to this, the IRA informer also claimed that Nicky Kehoe had been involved in the kidnapping. Kehoe was famous for being a member of Sinn Fein and the party's councilor for Dublin. He was an example of the blurred lines that existed between the Republicans' legitimate and more criminal wings. O'Callaghan even went as far as to name Bobby McNamara as being involved, mentioning that the man had been charged with casing the farm and providing information on how to break into Ballymany, a surprisingly easy job.

Providing names for a criminal act is never likely to put the author in too many people's good graces. For many years, Sean O'Callaghan has been denounced by his former IRA colleagues (some of whom undoubtedly do not wish him well) and had his veracity doubted by the public. Some have claimed that he is an attention seeker, publishing information on some of Ireland's most distressing times in order to make a quick bit of money. Others have suggested that there is no smoke without fire and point to evidence such as the code names mentioned by Peter Thompson. Pieces of evidence such as this could well be rumors that were passed along to O'Callaghan through his Ira contacts, information which he elaborated on when writing his book. It does, however, provide a decent foundation for his version of events.

As told by Sean O'Callaghan, the kidnapping of Shergar was bundled to the extreme. The horse was killed hours after the operation. The gang, it seems, had no idea just how highly strung, temperamental, and demanding a thoroughbred racehorse would be. They severely overestimated their abilities to keep the animal calm. Shergar was "shot dead" just hours after leaving Ballymany, after reacting furiously to being put in the trailer. In a rage, the horse hurt his leg, adding to the maddened behavior. Unable to call a vet (who would surely recognize the world's best known racehorse) and unable to treat the animal themselves, the kidnappers shot Shergar there and then. As O'Callaghan mentions in his book, the entire operation was a "total cock-up." Furthermore, the IRA informant mentions that the horse is buried within 100 miles of the stables where he lived, while the motivation for the crime is given as the IRA hoping to provide themselves with funds for better weapons.

In the aftermath of the publishing of O'Callaghan's book, a rumor emerged that the group had been so embarrassed by their failures that not even the IRA informant himself had been told the entire story. It was said that the decision to kidnap Shergar had been made by the Army council, the ruling body of the Provisional IRA. The kidnapping of Shergar was the work of a special operations unit within the IRA whose purpose was to raise money for the rest of the organization. This kidnapping was to be the first of many such enterprises. A middle-man who had been closely entwined with one of the kidnappers was attributed as the source of the rumor, and his account maintains that the gang had been assured that they would be guaranteed safe passage all the way north to a farm on the border with Northern Ireland. They had even organized a vet to be taken with them, should anything happen to the horse. This vet – for reasons unknown – pulled out of the kidnapping at the last minute. It might have been a bout of nerve or guilt, and there was even the suggestion that the vet's wife had gotten wind of the plans and warned him away. But whatever the reason, he was not there when the horse was supposedly injured. Despite the safe passage being guaranteed, the money-raising venture plunged into failure when the kidnap victim was hurt.

As well as the stories of the vet who backed out of the kidnapping, there are those who have put forward a very different theory. While most people have come to accept the line that Shergar worked himself into a frenzy and injured himself, there are those who paint a different picture of the night. According to this theory, the Army Council themselves realized that the four days of negotiations were really going nowhere. With the owners unwilling to pay the full sum, their kidnap victim was as good as worthless. They needed to cut Shergar loose. But rather than simply releasing him back to the owners, they took the decision to have the horse shot. They assumed that the police would now be searching every hidden corner in Ireland for any trace of the horse and that any clue might lead the investigators right to their door. The Army Council could not be implicated. Shergar could not be allowed to live. As such, they took the decision to kill the horse. Mallon himself supposedly ordered that the horse be shot.

Furthermore, we have an in-depth story of how this supposedly happened. On Mallon's orders, two men were sent to the stable where Shergar was being kept. They took machine guns with them. As they entered the horse's living quarters, the men opened fire. It was a bloody death, the walls painted with the blood. A machine gun in a closed space can tear a body to shreds. The bullets cut through the horse like so many hot knives through so much butter. As the walls, floors, and ceilings were stained with their handiwork, the men swore and cursed and discovered that the horse was not even dead. Unleashing further rounds into the champion racehorse, they eventually managed to put the animal down. The stable afterwards was like something from a nightmare. For some people, this version of the story is too horrific to believe. But as we have seen, there are conflicting accounts, even from those within the supposedly guilty IRA.

If we are to believe that the IRA was responsible, then it seems that they managed to badly miscalculate what needed to be done. Though there had been some successes with the kidnapping of wealthy individuals in the past, with their friends and families members appealing for their return on television, this had generally brought with it pretty bad publicity for the kidnappers. As far back as the Lindbergh baby, few kidnappers had ever received a warm response from the public. This was bad enough when it was some unknown rich person, but to kidnap a national treasure such as Shergar painted the criminals in the worst possible light. People were furious. People were scared. People were confused. Nobody, it seemed, came out of the situation with what they wanted, least of all the general public. Even those who possessed Republican sympathies were seemingly quick to condemn such as act, if it had indeed been carried out by the IRA. In the burgeoning age of PR and image management, this was a serious misstep. That the horse was seemingly dead just served to make matters much, much worse.

But was the IRA truly to blame? Despite the wealth of material (including Sean O'Callaghan's book) that places Kevin Mallon's name front and center with regards to the kidnapping, the man himself has always denied being involved. In addition, no official branch of the IRA has ever claimed responsibility for the act. For a group that has always been quick to attach itself to even the worst bombings, this should be seen as significant. Furthermore, no one had ever been arrested in connection with the kidnap of Shergar. As well as Kevin Mallon, Nicky Kehoe has stringently denied any involvement and has cast doubt on Sean O'Callaghan's version of events. To drive his point home, Kehoe references the fact that O'Callaghan was working for both sides at the time, seemingly keen to paint the informant as an untrustworthy man.

There are examples of the IRA being embroiled in kidnapping cases. Even after the Shergar incident, people such as Galen Weston were targeted. Weston was a Canadian businessman who was in Ireland in 1983. There was an attempt to kidnap him and hold him to ransom, though this ultimately failed. The IRA did not give up, however, and succeeded in their attempts to kidnap Don Tidey, one of Weston's executives. Tidey spent three weeks with his captors before being found in the woods alive. It is suggested that the same people who tried and failed in the kidnapping of Shergar were behind the attempts on Weston and Tidey. Interestingly, Kehoe and one of his associates, Gerry Fitzgerald, were arrested, tried, and convicted for the attempted kidnapping of Galen Weston, though he denied being involved with the Shergar case.

Those who try to make enquiries in County Leitrim today will be met with silence. Trying to uncover the truth about the crime in that county is incredibly tough, with none of the residents seemingly willing to talk to journalists or investigators. It is thought that Ballinamore in County Leitrim is a town that holds many secrets, not just related to this case. But no one there wishes to talk. Reporters have even been warned against hanging around the town too long after people begin to realize that they're looking into the Shergar case. There is a pointed though largely unspoken threat against those who ask questions in the town. The farms throughout the area are said to be under the ownership of those with Republican sympathies, and the deep bogs out near Aughnasheelan would be the ideal place in which to bury a body. There are local rumors throughout the area that this is indeed where Shergar was laid to rest, though no one has gone on the record to say as much.

Untying the knot of Shergar's kidnapping often feels like trying to countenance rumors and gossip. Often, people will present adamant claims that they know exactly what happened on that night, only for their version to contradict other accounts. Sometimes, their stories are easily proven false. Other times, there is a distinct weight of possibility behind the stories, and one is left wondering as to the source of the information. But in trying to track it down, the trail goes cold beyond the stage of whispers and discussions in bars. Even the more reliable sources, those published in books and newspapers, have their failings.

Finding the Truth

So how can we figure out what exactly happened during the kidnapping? Was the IRA involved? That seems almost certain. Did Shergar die during the first few hours? That's a very real possibility. Why were both sides of the kidnapping almost comically inept? It's impossible to tell. As we move deeper and deeper into the mystery, versions of the story begin to become conflicted and disprove one another. At this point, we have to simply assess the individual versions on their own merits. But where should we start? How exactly can we come close to cracking this coldest of cases?

The interest in the case of Shergar's kidnapping was global. To that extent, a journalist named Nick Harris was dispatched from a Japanese newspaper to try and uncover more information. Like Ireland, Japan is a country with a great love of the sport, so the Japanese took a strong interest in the case of the missing horse. The paper, Hokkaido Shimbun (sometimes referred to as Doshin) started by securing an interview with the man who claimed to be best informed on the kidnappers' side of the story, Sean O'Callaghan. The interview was arranged to happen just before the release of O'Callaghan's tell-all book, at a time when the author was fully aware that his life was in legitimate danger. Not only had he turned against the IRA and informed on them, but he also was now willing to publish a book filled with his story. For the Irish Republican Army, this was seemingly unacceptable.

Due to the precarious nature of O'Callaghan's position, Harris had to arrange the interview through a contact. Before it could take place, the interviewee conducted a thorough examination of Harris's past, to ensure that Harris wasn't being sent by the IRA. When he was satisfied that Harris was an authentic journalist, O'Callaghan travelled to the Doshin offices and began to talk about the part of the book that seemed the most interesting: the Shergar kidnapping.

During the course of the interview, the informant remained vague as to the exact location of the horse's body. He would only say that it lay somewhere in County Leitrim, to the north. This encompassed a huge area, one with rolling hills and inaccessible peat bogs. Anything other than a cursory search of this countryside was simply out of the question, something which O'Callaghan surely knew. It is likely that O'Callaghan knew just how invested the public was in the story of Shergar. With the publication of his book in the near future, drumming up attention by claiming to know the truth behind the case was a charge often levied against O'Callaghan. Did he really have inside information of the night in question? Was he actually there? Had he simply heard rum ours and pieced together the story himself, keeping everything vague enough that he would never be challenged on the truth?

Harris seemed aware of the difficulties in verifying the story. He talked to a number of anonymous ex-IRA members about the incident and seemed to get some kind of confirmation. The three people he talked to had definite connections to the organization, and they agreed that the IRA had indeed kidnapped Shergar and that the horse was definitely dead. This seemed to be in line with every single source on the subject, and it became apparent that all parties involved were resigned to the death of Shergar. The final word on the matter came when the Aga Khan and the other owners released a joint statement on the 6th of February, 1984. In the release, they described the chances that their horse was still alive as being "remote." Everyone, it seemed, believed that Shergar was dead.

Despite the resigned nature of the case, mysteries abounded. Due to the fact that no one was ever charged, the case of Shergar's kidnapping and death became a legend. So tightly was the story entwined with the history of Ireland that the public was always keen for more information. This was not just limited to the Emerald Isle. Across the sea in Britain, people were also wrapped up in the strangeness of the tale. Despite the differences that might have arisen from the Troubles, there was a reverence for Shergar, the legendary racehorse, and a hope that his kidnappers would be brought to justice. Even beyond Europe, there was an interest in the story, as we have seen through the involvement of Nick Harris. Despite Shergar's death being all but confirmed, people were still fascinated. They wanted to know the truth.

To that end, a journalist named David Ashforth published a series of articles in 2008 that recaptured the mystery surrounding the incident. His review of the case is useful, benefitting from the broad scope of hindsight. Published in the Racing Post, one of Britain's most popular sports outlets, the series not only reiterated the legendary achievements of Shergar, but also continued the investigation into the circumstances surrounding his death. Ashforth was able to uncover several shreds of the story that had escaped the investigators back in 1983. For example, he revealed that on the 12th of February, four days after the kidnapping, Stan Cosgrove walked into the Crofton Airport Hotel in Dublin. Cosgrove was Shergar's vet, trusted with the horse's wellbeing. When he entered the hotel, he walked up to the desk and gave his name as Johnny Logan. For those who are not aware, Johnny Logan was the name of the man who had won the Eurovision Song Contest three years earlier. A frequent contestant, his name was synonymous with the competition. The name was a code established by the kidnappers. They had insisted that whoever walked up to the front desk have no connection with the kidnapped horse. Cosgrove's presence (under a false name) was in direct defiance of the instructions passed along by the kidnappers.

Cosgrove walked to the front desk of the hotel and asked whether there had been any messages left for him. Just like Peter Thompson's efforts, the communications between the kidnappers and the owners were typically short and to the point. They were conducted using public telephones. When he was told that there was no message to be had, "Johnny Logan" left a contact number where he could be reached. It was the number for the Ballymany stables. Cosgrove ate a breakfast (perhaps to disguise his presence in the hotel) and left.

Just a few hours later, a phone rang. It was not in Ballymany, nor was it in the Crofton Airport Hotel. Instead, it was the phone on the desk of the Aga Khan's office in Paris. It was the kidnappers, identifying themselves with the familiar code name King Neptune. Allegedly, the kidnappers had called the hotel and been provided with a number. They sounded furious. There was to be nothing to do with the horse, the man shouted. Not Cosgrove, not the number for the stables. All of these could link a simple phone call to the hotel with the kidnapping. Rather than Cosgrove (or "Johnny Logan"), the kidnappers demanded that the owners send another person. Someone "clean." Someone with no connection to the horse. Should this person fail to appear, then the owners would never see the horse again.

A short time later, the kidnappers called again. This time their demands were equally as strict. They insisted that one person – and one person only – be chosen to hold negotiations on behalf of the owners' syndicate. This one person needed to be on the phone in exactly five minutes. When it became clear that it would not be possible to reach a decision on such a person, they magnanimously extended the deadline to an hour. To further confirm their serious intent, the kidnappers also threatened to kill Cosgrove and anyone whom he had contacted should any of the kidnappers be caught. Right now, the caller confirmed, the horse was alive. The man on the other end of the phone line told the Aga Khan's office that his word was important. If he said Shergar was alive, then Shergar was alive. If he said Shergar was dead, then they could begin the mourning process. The call finished with the kidnapper asking Cosgrove whether he really understood exactly who he was dealing with.

As Ashforth tells it, the next step of the conversation involved an envelope that was left at the desk of the Rosnaree Hotel in Drogheda. Sealed inside the envelope was a photograph of the horse's head alongside a copy of the previous day's Irish News. It was designed to show that the horse was indeed alive and well. However, there were doubts about the picture. While there was no mistaking the identity of the horse – the distinctive white mark across the face was iconic and clearly Shergar – the photo did little to show whether the animal was actually alive. It could well have been a dead horse, posed to appear alive for a photograph. This picture divided people reviewing the case, with various sides using it to confirm their version of events.

After receiving the photograph, the owners' syndicate and those acting on their behalf were split. The Aga Khan was one of the group who was unwilling to pay the ransom, though there were definitely certain owners who simply wished to see the horse returned, no matter what the cost. When King Neptune phoned again, the person elected to speak informed him that not every member of the syndicate was happy that Shergar was alive. The photo was not enough. The response was short. If the owners were not satisfied, the caller said, "That's it." The call ended abruptly and the dial tone rang out around the room. The dull flat tone was as good as a death knoll for the champion horse. Whether or not the picture really did depict a living, breathing Shergar, he would never be seen again.

Ashforth's version of events painted the owners' syndicate as being divided. They were split on whether to pay the ransom and – with moves such as sending Cosgrove to the hotel – were fully capable of causing enough problems for themselves. The kidnappers in this version of events were brutally efficient. They were keeping tabs on those who interacted with them and were able to provide proof of the horse's status. But this photograph – key to Ashforth's version of events – was a major point of division. Which side of the story did it really confirm? Was the horse alive or simply arranged to give the appearance of life? Though the King Neptune of Ashforth's articles appeared to be cold, calculating, and unwilling to be messed around by the owners, it could well have been that the horse was already dead and the abrupt manner was simply a diversionary tactic, a means of extracting money from the owners despite the fact that the horse was already dead.

Just as with O'Callaghan's book, the series of articles that Ashforth published in the Racing Post demonstrated the public's hunger for the truth as well as the cloak-and-dagger nature of the operation. There was duplicity on both sides, with enough maneuvering room for any version of events to emerge as the truth. It seemed that most versions of the Shergar story functioned as a kind of Rorschach test, allowing the reader to manipulate and alter the story to fit their own version of events. The key to solving the mystery was to examine as many possible versions and to notice the correlations and contrasts. By probing through every single case, perhaps it would be possible to discern the raw facts. As with completing a jigsaw puzzle, it helped to find the corner pieces, then the edges, and then move on to the rest. Now that the mystery was deepening, it was reasonable to hope that the truth would emerge from the fog.

A Bungled Operation

A repeated theme throughout the entire affair was that mistakes were made by both sides. Regardless of which story or interpretation you chose to believe, there was no doubt that many attempts to resolve the situation were bungled or otherwise compromised. Looking back over the case, it was easy to spot certain errors and wonder what might have happened if the right decision had been made. Instead, all that was left was a string of hypothetical situations in which the twisted version of events was as much a string of calamities as it was a true tragedy. But what could have been done differently?

One of the major offenders in this regard was the police force. In numerous times throughout the story, the kidnappers were adamant that the police should not be involved. However, some of the first phone calls placed on the night of the kidnapping went to high ranking government officials. It was only a matter of time before the police became involved. As soon as it became clear that the IRA might be implicated, the authorities had little choice but to insert themselves into the resolution. With a figure as public as Shergar and an organization as dangerous as the IRA, demanding no police involvement seemed like a pipe dream for the kidnappers. For the criminals, not only was there the possibility that they might be caught and tried for their actions, but there was the distinct chance that the operation might be a bad PR move for their cause. With the public so fond of Shergar, any harm caused to the animal would not reflect well on the IRA. It would also bring unwanted attention on their operations, at a time when the Troubles were the organization's primary focus. They didn't need police attention from a bungled kidnapping and were adamant that the authorities should not be involved.

But the police were involved. For better or worse, the list of police failures during the Shergar investigation made one wonder whether they were any help at all. Leading the investigation was Chief Spt. Murphy, commonly known as "Spud." Murphy would eventually become a key figure in the media's portrayal of the story but not for the right reasons. He came to represent everything that the police got wrong during the case. This was perhaps summed up in the one quote that was passed into common parlance in Ireland and Great Britain, becoming a repeated and legendary phrase across all forms of media. When asked about the investigation, he responded with the phrase; "A clue? Now that is something we haven't got."

The phrase is telling. The police soon found themselves hampered by the sheer lack of leads that they possessed. There were no clues, no hints, and no trails to follow. It got to the point where the police force even began to employ psychic investigations to give them a supernatural insight into the whereabouts of Shergar. But it all came to naught. Very quickly, the media took to referring to Murphy as Inspector O'Clouseau, playing on the name of the hapless detective in the Pink Panther comedy films.

In general police work, however, James Murphy was a respected figure. He had risen through the ranks and had earned the position he attained. His record was good, and he had the backing of the rest of the force. The mockery in the press might well have been a reflection on just how little there was to go on. Without any clues to report or any progress to detail, the media turned instead into mocking the ineptitude of the police. The peculiarities and out-of-the-box thinking displayed by Murphy became the only forward-moving aspects of the case and were all the papers had to print.

Indeed, the police were hampered by the fact that the kidnappers had an eight-hour head start. The first phone call was placed to the police at 4 o'clock in the morning on the 9th of February, a full eight hours after the kidnappers had first arrived at Ballymany. This gave the criminals a huge head start. Such a massive time advantage meant that the kidnappers could have been almost anywhere in Ireland by the time the authorities were mobilized, even though they were towing a heavy horse trailer. Already at a disadvantage, Murphy and his men found themselves chasing ghosts in the early hours of the morning.

It is perhaps because of James Murphy's rough treatment in the press that he consistently refused to publish his story. Though his first-hand account of the tale was no doubt of huge interest, he dismissed offers of as much as a quarter of a million pounds to give his version of events. Apparently, he made a promise to himself never to sell the story, and it was a promise he stuck to. Still, the very idea that there was an unheard side to this story just demonstrated how deep the rabbit hole went.

Communication, it seemed, became a very real problem. Many of the most bungled aspects of the case were down to simple errors in imparting ideas. For some people, the blame for this could be laid at the feet of Ghislain Drion, the Frenchman who had been appointed as Stud Manager at Ballymany. Drion's French accent perplexed and confused the kidnappers, adding an extra layer of difficulty that made initial exchanges terse. But his failure to communicate properly with the police, with the media, and even with those around him meant that Drion has a great deal to answer for.

Drion's role in the case was examined in great detail in a book by Colin Turner, a reporter for the London Broadcasting Company. During the course of writing the book, the author offered a reward for any information that might lead to the location of the kidnapped horse. Rather than a ransom for Shergar's return, he hoped the financial inceptive would encourage people to come forward. The approach was not entirely successful, and it did land him an interview with Drion, the results of which formed the backbone of the book. The trick to getting the interview had been to seek to discuss the reward with the owners' syndicate. Turner had hoped to rally the owners into putting up the cash. Since all communications went through Drion, Turner came up against the same figure every time. After repeated failed attempts, the journalist was pleased that − if a reward was out of the question − that at least Drion would provide an interview. The Frenchman agreed. Turner explained that he hoped the discussion would "break down [the] wall of silence" that had been built up around Ballymany. In 1984, Turner released the book titled In Search of Shergar, in which he spent a lot of time interviewing Drion.

When Colin interviewed Drion, it was at Ballymany Stud. As the two sat down, Drion began to offer up his version of the story. One of the very first allegations put forward by the journalist to the Stud Manager was that the lack of communication with the press and the police was a shining example of how the owners were "cocking things up."

For the police, the lack of information was a real problem. James Murphy had discovered that information was hard to come by in the case. When he sat down with Drion and the other owners and representatives, he was given very little to work with. This was backed up by Captain Sean Berry, another person who worked on the case. The only material they were given came from Stan Cosgrove, the vet. Drion should have been the man to act as the line of communication between all of the parties, as open discussions and sharing are crucial when it comes to kidnap cases. But Drion seemed incapable of managing this, a charge that – while he might not accept – he seemed reticent to dismiss. Similarly, the lack of security that the kidnappers encountered at Ballymany was put down to failings on the part of Drion. Just a few weeks before Shergar was taken, he had rejected the addition of a brand new security system that had been priced at just £1000. That price, he felt, was too high. At the time of the kidnapping, the only security in place was a broken CCTV camera that did not even have tape ready to go in the machine. According to Colin Turner's book, the stables themselves were unkempt and untidy. Drion, it seems, was doing a poor job of managing the facility and made it very easy for the kidnappers to go about their task.

Communication from all quarters was difficult. Even the famous Aga Khan was hard to get hold of. Seemingly showing a complete lack of interest in the kidnapping, the esteemed millionaire owner did not even travel to Ireland in the months following the disappearance of his prized racehorse. This perceived lack of interest cause consternation amongst the public. Why was the owner not even concerned about the missing horse? Why should the public campaign for Shergar's safe return when the owner himself did not seem to give a damn? The Aga Khan succinctly communicating his concerns or simply appearing next to Captain Murphy at a press conference could have been a huge PR boost to the investigation and could have assured everyone that they were pulling in the right direction, but 'twas not to be.

Any kind of communication with the police could have been a huge help. And it was not as though the authorities were not clued in on the idiosyncrasies of horseracing. Captain Berry, for example, was the chairman of the Irish Thoroughbred Breeders Association at the time and a key figure in the investigation. He had been one of the first people to receive a call on the night that Shergar went missing. A former Army officer now working in the equestrian world, he should have been an ideal go-between for the owners and the police. There were few who understood the importance and value of Shergar better than he did. Berry maintained that the operation organized by the police force in Dublin ran alongside (but rarely in partnership with) the local police force in County Kildare. Each group was unaware of what the other was doing, of any progress that was being made, or any actions that were being taken. The lack of communication was a huge flaw. Each of the two teams hoped to be the force to crack the case and so be able to take the credit. Rather than working together, they competed. It became so extreme that even Berry's home and work phone lines were tapped, while he was told not to share any of his information with Chief Murphy.

But Berry was one of the more tenacious investigators. Not as interested in the glory and publicity that were attached to the case, he was marked by his difference from the rest of the force. Based in the Equine Research Centre in Johnstown, he and his team were one of the lowest profile outfits working on the case. They received calls and tip offs from some of the strangest sources. Even in March, on the holiday of St Patrick's Day, Berry and his team were fielding calls from clairvoyants and religious people who believed that they possessed supernatural knowledge of Shergar's location. The sheer volume of calls from dubious sources was maddening for those given the task of answering the phones. Once Berry and his team were able to separate the few good slivers of information from the huge amount of bad, they were left with a few slight leads.

Chief among these were the people Berry referred to as "subversives." This was a code word for those who worked for the IRA, and they were thoroughly vetted before they were allowed to provide information. According to the information that Berry received from these individuals, not only were the police keeping tabs on him, but members of the IRA had also been given the job of tailing the former Army captain in his day-to-day life.

Berry was not without his critics, however. One of the most lambasted ideas he put forward concerned the reward. He was prepared to offer a quarter of a million pounds for Shergar's safe return. This was criticized by those who worried that it would lead to the targeting of other racehorses, as well as the perception that the kidnappers were potentially being rewarded. Berry countered this with the admission that the money was never in place to pay anyone who had come forward and that the disagreements and communication failures on behalf of the owners meant that – even if there had been money available – it would never have been paid out. In Berry's view, Shergar was likely already dead by the time his investigation took place, and the so-called "subversives" he encountered were probably just trying to make money from the rumors and hearsay that was spreading through their social circles. In spite of this belief, Berry still hoped for as much information as possible and did whatever he could to encourage people to come forward with any leads.

One method involved visiting radio shows and mentioning the reward money while on the air. Though it was rarely announced through official channels, this idea of a large sum soon worked its way into the public's consciousness. This had the desired effect in March, when a caller phoned a radio station and identified himself using a code name – "Rugby." According to the caller, if there was indeed a financial reward available, then negotiations could begin. In response, Berry asked for proof that Shergar was actually alive and well, considering most people assumed the horse to be dead by this point.

Rugby did not get in touch until May. During the months in between, the stressed-out and tired Berry had taken a short holiday to the Canary Islands. When he came back, the phone call thrust him right back into the case. Berry was told to travel to the Hotel Keadeen, located in Newbridge, where he would discover a letter that had been placed there and was currently waiting for him, addressed to "Davies." Once he picked up the letter, a phone call would be placed. After this, Berry was told that he would be collected from the hotel at two o'clock the next afternoon, and he would be taken to see the horse.

The former Army captain agreed. Colluding with the police, he allowed them to fit a tracking device to his person. When the phone rang the next day at two o'clock, he was asked whether the money was ready to go. Berry responded with furious indignation. No, he shouted, the money was not ready to go. It would remain as such until he was furnished with proof that Shergar really was alive. It was two days before the caller was in touch again.

This time, Berry was told that he would need to go to Kildare, travel to a certain phone booth and await a call. This was done, and when he picked up the handset, a voice on the other end informed Berry about the arrangements that had been made. Shergar was alive, and Berry would be allowed to visit him. As a response, Berry put forward the idea that Cosgrove, Shergar's vet, should accompany him, reiterating the importance of the horse's well-being before any discussion about money could take place. After he hung up, there were no more phone calls.

The reasoning for Cosgrove's presence was not a silly as it might have sounded. Though the vet's presence in negotiations had previously been a point of contention for those claiming to be the kidnappers, he played a vital role. Berry was well aware that the insurance policy attached to the racehorse covered death but did not cover theft. Therefore, he wanted Cosgrove to accompany him in order to verify that Shergar was either dead or alive. If the insurance company was to pay out, then they would need the horse's vet to confirm the death.

But the caller seemed spooked. The communications broke down and died after that demand. It might well have become clear that both sides were bluffing. Berry had no intention of putting up the money that had been mentioned as a reward, while it could well have been the case that the caller was taking a chance and trying to con the owners out of any financial reward that he could have gotten without having to provide proof. To borrow an old phrase, he could well have been trying to flog a dead horse. As both sides began to realize that they were unable to get what they wanted, the communications broke down once again. As throughout the case, brokered information from both parties collided and caused problems for everyone involved. Shergar was still missing and was now presumed dead.

There was one final twist in the tale. Roughly a month after Berry's last attempt to communicate had failed, Cosgrove found himself talking to a horse dealer in County Clare named Denis Minogue. He was introduced to the man via a police officer, who claimed that the horse dealer had quite a story to tell. Cosgrove detailed his story in an article published in the Irish Times, in which he recounted Minogue's tale. Allegedly, a hood was placed over the man's head, and he driven out into the countryside on the pretext of seeing Shergar. Once he had arrived, the hood was removed and − in the unknown location − Minogue was convinced that he saw the horse. Alive. Minogue repeated the feat and was allowed to see the horse on two separate occasions. To prove his story, he provided Cosgrove with details and observations that were convincing enough that the vet bought the story. In fact, he became so convinced that Denis Minogue was telling the truth that he gathered together £80,000 of his own money and offered it as a reward for the horse's safe return.

It was deemed to be enough. It seemed as though the £80,000 was an acceptable amount. Cosgrove, Minogue, and the policeman (a man named Keirnions) were given the arrangements on how they might be able to pay the money to the kidnappers. The fee was to be paid in cash. It was collected and counted by Keirnions and placed into a black bag. This bag was then placed into the boot of the car, alongside a £10,000 "finder's fee" for Denis Minogue for his assistance. The car was then driven out to Ardnacruisha in County Clare and parked in a remote location. The men left the car on foot and walked away to a specific point, just as they had been instructed. They left behind the money in the boot of Minogue's car where it would be collected in exchange for Shergar's safe return. When they walked back to the vehicle, they discovered that the money had simply vanished. There was no information suggesting how the racehorse might be returned. The exchange was an utter failure. According to Cosgrove, Keirnions described the shock of the disappearance of the money as being similar to the shock at the death of his father. Though the vet had been convinced of the policeman's legitimacy earlier, major doubts had arisen by the time he wrote the article.

Indeed, the police officer was later arrested. The abject failure of the exchange led many to believe that it had all been a ruse. Keirnions was investigated by the police, was then suspended and sacked, before leaving to open a small hotel out on the west Irish coast. Minogue continued to insist that Shergar was alive, claiming that he had seen the horse as late as August in 1983. Cosgrove, despite his initial acceptance, seemed to have swung the other way. By the time the article appeared in the Irish Times, he was resigned to the fact that Shergar likely died in the days following the kidnapping, if not earlier.

The failure of Cosgrove's exchange was perhaps the most obvious of all the bungled attempts at retrieving Shergar from the kidnappers. Time and time again, a lack of communication between the owners, the investigators, and those who hoped to see the horse returned meant that mistake after mistake was made. These were costly. Not only did men such as Cosgrove lose a large amount of their own money, but people such as Berry placed themselves into threatened positions, chasing the hope that they might be able to retrieve the horse. Time, energy, and resources were all poured down the drain as those involved failed to communicate properly. While it was unlikely Shergar would ever have been returned alive, the long list of failures adds a distinct "what if" element to the case. It certainly made it difficult to apportion blame for the loss of the racehorse, especially at a time when so many people had made so many errors.

But what of the kidnappers? Though we mostly have the story of those involved on the owners' side, those who carried out the kidnapping are perhaps the most interesting of all. Though there is a general acceptance that the IRA was behind the operation, there are those who think otherwise. In the next chapter, we will look into those responsible for springing Shergar from his stable and will look into whether the Irish Republican Army really were to blame.

.

Whodunit

One of the most intriguing aspects of the Shergar case is the way in which it is able to uniquely combine all of the elements of a cold case, a kidnapping, and a conspiracy theory all at once. The geopolitical situation in Ireland at the time meant that there were far more important events occurring, though few felt as monumental or as emotionally taxing as the kidnapping of a racehorse. Because of this, it should probably be no surprise to see that so many people have rushed to fill in the void of information with their own theories. In this chapter, we will seek to establish a few of the more outlandish theories, a few of the lesser-known variations, and even the commonly accepted versions of how Shergar was taken, why he was taken, and what became of the horse.

One of the strangest theories related to the case is the idea that the owners' syndicate themselves could have staged the kidnapping. As a means of backing up this theory, proponents put forward a few select facts. Firstly, they point to the idea that Shergar's career as a racehorse was waning. Now in retirement, there had been suggestions that his career as a stud were not going to plan. Though the first year at Ballymany had raised nearly £3 million, there were doubts over his future earning potential. With people having bought into the horse when he was valued at £10 million, this presented a worrying loss of money. The insurance claim that could be made if the horse was killed would be a potential way in which they could have made back their money. Thanks to the Troubles, they had a shadowy organization in place ready to blame for the crime. The way the world saw it, the owners syndicate would be innocent, and the money would be a sure thing. Added to this idea are a number of factors. Why was the Aga Khan so reluctant to fly into Ireland during such an important time? Why were the owners seemingly so reluctant to put up their own money to have Shergar returned? Why was there such an inability to collaborate and chase down the kidnappers? Perhaps it was because they did not want to be caught?

But this theory falls down when examined closely. As we have seen, the insurance policy was dependent on the horse being dead if it were to pay out. This was why Captain Berry insisted on the vet Cosgrove being taken along to a meeting. If all that was required was for the horse to be killed, there were far easier ways in which to stage a death than such an elaborate kidnapping. Furthermore, the fact that nobody was ever recovered puts the insurance claim in real jeopardy. Without proof of death, there were many more difficulties facing those who wanted to make a claim. Added to this, the sheer scale of the conspiracy was massive. The Aga Khan was not the only owner. Instead, 40 shares had been sold, meaning that there was a huge number of people who would have had to have been in on the secret if it was to work. What's more, there is no evidence that Shergar's stud career was in jeopardy. After the first year at Ballymany, an even greater number of mares had been lined up to visit Shergar. His reputation alone was enough to pay his value several times over. While the theory was attractive to those who enjoy a conspiracy, it relied too greatly on chance and everybody involved keeping quiet for all of these years, as well as dismissing the work that linked actual suspects to the kidnapping. It was easily put aside.

There is a similar theory that suggests Shergar was stolen with his racing abilities in mind. Rather than being killed, the death of the horse was only put forward in order to keep people distracted. Once the furor over the kidnapping had died down, Shergar could reappear on the remote Irish farm where he had been kept captive. Unleashed under a different name (and presumably, with his distinctive colorings disguised), the horse would be entered into a small race at huge odds. With 50-1 not being unknown for a new entrant without any history, the kidnappers could then place a bet on Shergar at massive odds and make a huge amount of money. Repeat this trick a few times, and the ransom fee would be more than paid.

This theory also falls apart when examined closely. First, Shergar was a national icon. Had he been entered in any race, then he would instantly have been recognized. Second, the horse alone is not the only part of winning a race. He had to be cared for and conditioned, he had to be trained and ridden properly. Shergar benefited from the very best in professional care and preparation. Entering him into a random race after a year or two of being out of the sport would by no means guarantee a victory, especially when coming up against horses in the midst of a full and proper training regime. What's more, the chances of being able to place a suitably large bet at such long odds without attracting the attention of the authorities (and doing so repeatedly) would simply not be possible. Even in 1983, there was enough of a fraud investigation network in place so as to monitor betting irregularities of this nature. Put simply, it was a far too complicated and abstract plan ever to work in the real world.

So rather than taking Shergar to race, maybe the true purpose of kidnapping the horse was to benefit from his breeding potential. Now at stud, Shergar's profitability was well known. As the most expensive horse of the day, any foal bred from his stock was worth a pretty penny. If a kidnapper would be able to keep the horse in comfort, he could breed himself an army of thoroughbreds that would be worth huge amounts. But this theory belies one key factor about horse breeding. Reputation is everything. In order for a stud to be worth anything, he must have a reputation. Shergar's value lay in the fact that everyone knew who he was. Had he been anonymous and in possession of the exact same genes, he would be worth a fraction of his value. For a kidnapper, the only value to be made from breeding Shergar would come from people knowing that the kidnapper was in possession of the famous horse. If that were the case, then the authorities would immediately have become aware. In addition, horse breeding is not a fine art. Over thirty mares were paired with Shergar during his first year as a stud. The offspring were not thirty Derby winners. Instead, breeding can often come down to chance and luck as much as genetics. Kidnapping a horse for this purpose would be far from a sure way to make money.

In a slight alteration to this this, there had been the suggestion that Shergar might well have been kidnapped by a wealthy foreign owner. Typically, theories such as these suggest that some unnamed Middle Eastern Sheik saw Shergar and decided that he would want the horse for his own private breeding stock. Rather than hoping to sell the offspring or put the horse to stud, the mysterious figure simply hoped to breed the finest horses in the world for pleasure, perhaps entering the children in a race or two in the future. If they turned out to be champions, then all the better. If not, then Shergar would just become another expensive trinket, a play thing for the superrich, the non-acquirable asset that had been acquired by illegal means.

But this theory presented one key factor that becomes a repeated theme in this chapter: how could the horse have been transported out of the country? Any stud facility in Ireland of decent enough size or standard is a known quantity. It was not possible in such a small country for there to be a top secret breeding facility for the finest horses in the world. To get around this, the horse would have to have been shipped overseas. But this, the authorities agreed, would have been almost impossible. Trying to get the horse on a plane would have required a number of inspections and a raft of paperwork. No such inspections or paperwork were carried out or issued. To do so secretly would have required the chartering of a private jet (one capable of transporting a horse). No such planes were chartered. To sneak the animal out by boat would have required a slow and elaborate effort of getting a horse on to a ship and then keeping it alive and happy for a huge amount of time, all while at sea. It was, the experts seems to agree, an impossible job. Furthermore, it would have required the silence of everyone involved in the operation, which would have been a high number. Since no one came forward with anything resembling legitimate evidence of this happening, the theory can be dismissed with relative ease.

So where did that leave the story? Surprisingly, these are not the most outlandish theories. Though they might have seemed possibly true, they were the versions of events that provided little to nothing in the way of evidence. Thus, they were the theories that were quickly put to one side. What was the most outlandish? If someone told you that the kidnapping of the most famous racehorse in Ireland was carried out by the New Orleans Mafia, would you believe them?

This particular theory can be traced back to one man: Michel Gambet. Gambet was a minor player on the French horseracing circuit. As a bloodstock agent, he was involved in the breeding of horses and helping pair-up clients to ensure the birth of new animals with the best possible pedigree. An acquaintance of the Aga Khan, the story goes that he had in mind to purchase one of the man's horses. The horse he had in mind was named Vayraan. Though not as famous nor as successful as Shergar, it was well bred and worth money. Gambet believed he could turn a profit on Vayraan. The only problem was, he didn't have the money. He needed capital. The Aga Khan was willing to sell, but only at the right price. Desperate to see the deal go through, Gambet turned to America and, in particular, to the organized crime circuit in that most French part of the United States: New Orleans.

The story went that Michel Gambet turned to the New Orleans Mafia in a desperate attempt to raise the funds to buy the horse. He must have had a quick turnaround in mind, an easy profit. As such, you can imagine his horror when the deal collapsed. The money had already been spent. Gambet was unable to pay the crime syndicate their money back. The mafia decided that, rather than taking the non-existent cash from Gambet, they were instead owed a horse from the Aga Khan. But rather than kidnapping Vaynaar, they took Shergar instead. After everything went wrong. Michel Gambet was found dead in his car in December of 1983, the body abandoned somewhere in Kentucky. The reports seemed to put the cause of death as suicide, but the report from the official state medical examiner hinted that the bullet which had passed through the man's temple was almost certainly from a different caliber gun to the one found next to the body. The bullet was never recovered, however, so the investigation never really took off. Just as the fuss and bother over the missing racehorse was still raging in Ireland, the crime syndicate returned to their native land to let the whole thing blow over.

It was an interesting theory. However, there were a number of factors that seemed to contradict this version of events. First, if the New Orleans Mafia was familiar with the dealings of Michel Gambet, then they were likely familiar with his French accent. When the kidnappers struggled to comprehend the accent of Ghislain Drion, it seemed as though they had never heard such an accent before. For New Orleans mobsters, this is incredibly unlikely. Next, the theory overlooks all of the Irish involvement said to revolve around the case. Though mostly speculation, there was little doubt that there was a distinctly Irish quality to the crime, from the choice of target to the ease with which the perpetrators sank back into the mists. They seemed like local lads, aware of the implications of what they were doing. Finally, the strand of investigation was never pursued by anyone involved in the incident. Not only did the police not signal any intent to investigate New Orleans, but the Aga Khan, the man involved with Michel Gambet, saw no reason why the two incidents might be linked. It seemed more like the needless linking of two disparate crimes rather than a cohesive theory.

But the idea of the New Orleans Mafia was not the only time that suspicions had travelled over the Atlantic. A man named Wayne Murty, for example, was often linked with the kidnapping of Shergar. Murty was an American and a known rival of the Aga Khan. The two were far from friends, involved in a bitter feud that was not only well known, but well publicized. It could be traced back to a falling out in 1978, when the American had arranged to purchase some 56 horses from the esteemed owner, Marcel Boussac. Boussac was facing a collapsing business empire, and with bankruptcy rapidly approaching, he needed money fast. Murty saw the chance to get a great number of horses at a cut price. But before the deal could be finalized, a French court stepped in and ruled the sale illegal. Enter The Aga Khan. The Aga Khan arrived on the scene following the court ruling, set up a new deal, and pinched all 56 horses from under Murty's nose. The American was left furious. He accused the Aga Khan of using some level of influence in order to turn the deal against Murty. The two were known enemies in the years preceding the Shergar incident.

Is it conceivable, then, that Wayne Murty kidnapped and killed the Aga Khan's prized racehorse out of revenge over a soured business deal? Murty claimed that he certainly hated the man enough. In an interview given after the kidnapping, he admitted that he could well have kidnapped the horse due to the ongoing feud that raged between the two men. Getting back at the Aga Khan would have been something Murty relished. But, however, he finished the interview by denying any involvement. Never, he admitted, would he stoop so low. And he would certainly have been stupid to get involved in such a manner. A sworn public enemy of Shergar's owner, he would have been an obvious target for the investigation and would have found it difficult to dissuade himself from the attention of the police. Admitting to the possibility that he might have carried out the kidnapping in a media interview was hardly the behavior of a man who was trying to escape investigation. While he certainly had the motive, Wayne Murty would have had to have been either incredibly stupid or incredibly arrogant to kidnap Shergar.

So that brought back the most commonly suspected culprit: The Irish Republican Army. However, before plunging headlong into the detailed exploration of their involvement, there was another theory that implicates the IRA, but in a slightly different fashion. While the majority of thought suggests the kidnapping attempts as a means of raising funds, there have been those who have put forward the idea that the IRA might have been acting on the behalf of another major player on the world stage. Supposedly, that man's name is Colonel Gadhafi, the former leader of Libya.

The reasoning behind this more conspiratorial theory is not just financial. Rather, it comes down to religion. The title of the Aga Khan was not just ceremonial. For a certain section of the global Muslim community, it was also a spiritual position. The Aga Khan (and his predecessors who bore the same name) acted as the spiritual leader to a large community, one whom Colonel Gadhafi felt would be better suited under his direction. Added to this, Colonel Gadhafi's influence spread beyond North Africa. Known as an irritant to many global powers, he was constantly attempting to project his power and influence in many corners of the world. A promoter of many anti-government groups, Gadhafi was a known funder and accomplice of the Irish Republican Army. Implicated in the Lockerbie Bombing that occurred many years later, Gadhafi would have as pained a relationship with the British government as the IRA themselves. But this time, he sought to act against his spiritual enemy.

According to the often discredited theory, it is said that Colonel Gadhafi arranged for the IRA to kidnap the horse on his behalf. The thought process suggests that he viewed such an action as a way in which he could embarrass the Aga Khan, diverting more power and attention towards his own religious leadership. Shergar, the Aga Khan's most famous possession, should be taken away in a very public manner. Through his alleged funding of the IRA, Gadhafi had contacts within the organization, and it was they whom he called on when it came time to carry out the deed. Rather than acting for financial gain from the ransom fee, the IRA (it is suggested) were receiving their funding from the Libyan leader in exchange for a seemingly botched kidnap attempt.

This theory held little water. There was nothing to suggest that Colonel Gadhafi was even aware of the existence of Shergar, much less that he had arranged for the kidnap attempt. It seemed to be a way in which to complicate the already accepted notion that the IRA had conducted the operation purely for financial reasons. Disproving the theory was made all the more complex by the fact that Gadhafi was overthrown and his government demolished. Along with it, perhaps, went the last attempt at confirming any degree of involvement on behalf of the Libyan leader. While it might be farfetched, the theory certainly had its adherents. But there was still one prevailing notion that rose above and beyond the rest when it came to people's view of who kidnapped Shergar.

And that was the IRA, The Irish Republican Army. Throughout this book, their involvement has been treated as an assumption, something that could be taken from granted. In the wake of the kidnapping and the information that came to light in years later, there had almost always been an element of IRA involvement in every story. From Sean O'Callaghan's books to articles in the Racing Post, those who were interested in the kidnapping of Shergar would almost always turn to the IRA as being the chief suspects. But what was it that made them the foremost potential perpetrators of such an act in the minds of the public?

The majority of people – including the Aga Khan and a number of outspoken members of the owners syndicate – felt that the Irish Republican Army carried out the kidnapping in order to raise funds for their campaign. In 1983, with the Troubles at their peak and the fight against the British raging on and on, the IRA began to realize that they would need a greater level of funding in order to continue. The money came from all over the place. From international governments such as Libya, which felt a sympathy for the Irish cause, right up to regular Irish-Americans who passed around a hat in Boston bars and donated to "the Irish cause," often without realizing exactly what they were donating money to. But it was not always enough. The IRA needed weapons and resources. In order to acquire these items, they needed money. To people such as the Aga Khan, the kidnapping of a racehorse seemed an obvious IRA tactic.

It was certain that the IRA was involved in a number of kidnappings during the 1980s. As already mentioned in this book, the abduction of businessmen who were then ransomed back to their families was not unheard of. While it was not always successful, it was just one string in the fundraising bow, a quick way in which the organization could raise large sums of money. But as with many of the crimes carried out by the IRA, they would typically admit to their involvement. Technically, the IRA had been labelled as a terrorist organization. One of the key aspects of carrying out a terrorist attack was that it was important that people know exactly the reasoning behind the action. The Bishopsgate Bombing in London in 1993, for example, was marked by a phone call from the IRA before the bomb went off, and a communication afterwards confirmed the involvement of the organization. The group was not afraid of admitting to very serious crimes.

But the IRA never confirmed their involvement in the kidnapping of Shergar. While there have typically been confirmations of even the worst attacks, there has been no mention of the racehorse from official IRA channels. Similarly, a remarkably small number of former IRA members have sought to comment on the issue. Though people such as Sean O'Callaghan and others have said time and again that the IRA was involved in some fashion, these accounts are scattered and often contradictory. There remained little in the way of an official confirmation and nothing that could be taken for granted.

So why would the IRA not admit to their involvement, even three decades later? Following the peace agreements and the Good Friday truce that was signed in ensuing decades, there had been little motivation to delve too deeply into the events of the past. Many people in Ireland hoped simply to put the events behind them. There had been a tenuous peace. Finger pointing or confessions would only serve to dredge up bad memories of the past. In this respect, the lingering members of the IRA had little reason to come out and admit to their involvement in a crime. The investigation into the crime is closed, so to admit to it now would only potentially land people in jail. There seems a tacit agreement on both sides simply to let old matters die. Even though the IRA didn't take responsibility for the kidnapping was not to say that they were not involved. Rather, it simply demonstrated that the organization could gain little from being associated with the kidnapping. It would not further their political goals, it could land their members in jail, and it could reopen wounds that have been trying to heal in Ireland and Northern Ireland.

But one of the major lingering doubts over the involvement of the IRA was down to their strength as an organization. Thanks to their constant war against British involvement in Ireland, British Intelligence outfits were known to have infiltrated the IRA to a great extent. The number of informants and double agents was high (including men who were turned, such as Sean O'Callaghan). It seemed likely that if the IRA had plotted to kidnap as prominent a public figure as the legendary racehorse Shergar, that British Intelligence would have caught wind of the operation. Such an event would have given them an excellent precept for knocking on the doors of certain IRA strongholds and safe houses, causing strife to the organization as a whole. This did happen in various parts of Ireland, though seemingly not with the backing of the British Intelligence services. Furthermore, it seemed logical that if the British had known about the crime, then such a piece of information might have become better known. The Aga Khan was a prominent figure in Britain and was a friend of the Queen. It would not have been beyond the realm of possibility that the British Intelligence organizations would have attempted to solve the case using insider information.

For further details about the involvement and awareness of British Intelligence, there could be wait for the declassification of certain files. There was a time limit on just how long documents were able to remain secret, with new pieces of intelligence gathering being published each year the time from the original gathering period got longer and longer. The data related to the Troubles (and potentially to Shergar's kidnapping) had not yet passed the threshold for release. In addition to this, there was the possibility that the British were aware of the incident but did not want to act for fear of compromising their agents. They were fighting a bloody and brutal war, and the last thing they needed was for informants or moles to be uncovered by a botched kidnapping investigation. The official investigators had already shown themselves to be incompetent, so why would the British risk their agents and potentially risk victory in Northern Ireland? Again, the doubts and questions raised by some are met with counter arguments from others.

To some people, the IRA's failure to comment on the issue is damning in and of itself. Stan Cosgrove, the vet who was featured numerous times in this book, is one of those people. To him, the silence of the organization on the matter is simply proof of how deeply they were involved. According to Cosgrove, it was not long before those in the IRA realized that they had done "a repulsive thing to the Irish people." They had, in his opinion, grossly underestimated the outpouring of worry and grief that would result from the peril of a racehorse. But Shergar was an Irish icon, a tiny bit of joy for people to cling to in troubled times. Admitting to having been behind the disappearance and likely death of the horse would have been atrocious for the IRA, both at home and in America. As Cosgrove mentioned, the IRA could have killed someone like Margaret Thatcher and people would not have batted an eye. Because they chose such a beloved figure as Shergar, they soon realized their mistake and decided to keep quiet on the matter. A mixture of shame, bad publicity, and regret prevented the organization from taking credit. With his close proximity to the story, Cosgrove's opinion was certainly worth something. But what real evidence was there for the involvement of the IRA and how could such involvement be proven?

It can help when we are able to examine physical pieces of evidence. An excellent example of this was found just days after the negotiations with King Neptune had collapsed. During the month of February, after the police became officially involved, there was a search undertaken of the ground around Ballymany. The police combed the area in a desperate search for clues as to who had kidnapped Shergar. During this search, one officer came across a loaded sub-machine gun magazine. It was not something that was normally found on Ballymany's grounds and was immediately analyzed.

The investigators discovered that the magazine belonged to a Steyr-Daimler-Puch, an Austrian submachine gun that was typically associated with the Provisional Irish Republican Army. The men who had arrived at the stables on the fateful night had certainly been well-armed (as confirmed by Jim Fitzgerald), and this seemed to be something that had been left behind by the kidnappers. Though it contained no fingerprints or additional clues, the very nature of the magazine was enough to tie the crime to the IRA. Submachine guns were not easy to come by in Ireland, either now or during the 1980s. To acquire one, a person must have had contacts of a certain kind. The guns were known to be used by the IRA themselves, and it was certainly feasible that the group would use their more familiar weaponry when carrying out a kidnapping. The magazine was perhaps the only piece of physical evidence that the police recovered. Though it gave no real information, it was more than enough, for some people, at least, to tie the IRA to the kidnapping of Shergar.

There were huge numbers of stories from those involved in the IRA about what happened during the kidnapping of Shergar. Men such as Sean O'Callaghan were all too keen to speak about their involvement in the incident. Others later came forward and said that they either took part themselves or knew someone who did. Travel to any pub in Ireland in the decade following the kidnap, and you eventually got talking to someone who knew someone else who was there that night. After a few drinks more, they'd swear to being there themselves. Everyone had a story about how the IRA had done it. But the problem was that so many of these stories contradicted one another.

Trying to get a complete explanation of that night was almost impossible. It was known that there were close to nine men who arrived at Ballymany, which meant that nine men potentially knew the truth. But it seemed to stop there. The IRA was structured using a cell system. That is to say, there was no overarching command structure, no hierarchy of organization. Instead, the IRA collected people together in cells. These small "cells" of people would have no contact with one another and would not know about the other plans the IRA possessed. Instead, they would be given a task and told to go about it in isolation. This was a security measure. If one cell was caught or turned against the IRA, then they would have little information other than their own activities. In the case of Shergar's kidnappers, it is likely that the cell was given vague instructions and carried out their activities without the knowledge of anyone else in the organization.

Naturally, this would make getting an explanation difficult. Other than those in the cell, no one would have been present at the planning or execution stages. While these men undoubtedly conversed with friends and associates afterwards, they would likely pass on a subjective view of events and/or a slightly skewed one. Eventually, this would have led to a number of rumors and contradictory versions of the story floating around IRA social circles with the story changing each time. Eventually, it might reach someone like Sean O'Callaghan, who then published the version of events he had heard. Trying to establish the truth with so many different versions of the story floating around would have been almost impossible, like trying to find the truth at the heart of a fairy tale.

Because of this, the story of the Shergar kidnapping took on an almost mythical tone. There were just so many versions of what happened that night – who was there, when the horse died, how they entered the stables, what car were they driving, and so forth – that the truth may never be known. There was little to be gained from those who were there that night in telling their version of events. Not only would they face prosecution, but they would also have been pilloried in the press. There would have been little motivation for the IRA, who would have to own up to one of the more tragic events in Ireland's recent past. There was also very little motivation for the authorities to press forward with any investigation, lest they anger anyone involved and somehow compromise a fragile peace agreement. Instead, the only way in which the story of Shergar can be examined was to look at every single version of events and hope that a greater, firmer truth would make itself apparent, appearing out of the firmament.

Unless there is another version of the story. The links with the IRA were taken for granted, but there could have been a far more insidious truth, one which involved politicians and conspiracies. For those in the know, this version of events was called the Haughey Link.

The roots of this theory were far away from Ballymany, outside of Ireland altogether. The plot revolved around Wandsworth Prison. Found in London, the prison is capable of holding almost 2,000 inmates when at capacity, meaning it was one of the largest in the country at the time of the kidnapping. In 2007, however, a man imprisoned in Wandsworth wrote a letter. This was not just any man, and this was not just any letter. This was a man named John Hyde. Hyde was a notorious Irish mobster, one of the most heinous criminals in either Britain or Ireland. Serving time behind bars, he had been convicted by the government and given a lengthy sentence. But on the 11th of November, he decided to write a letter. The recipient of the letter was a man named Giovanni di Stefano, Hyde's lawyer. As the lawyer read through the letter, it became clear that his client was seeking advice. "I have a story," Hyde wrote, "and would like help in publishing it." According to the gangster, he was the last living person who had knowledge of exactly what happened to a racehorse named Shergar. Now, in 2007, Hyde was finally willing to reveal his side of the story and – more importantly – was willing to name names.

There was one more player; the man who gave this theory its name, Charles Haughey. Sometimes known by his nickname, "Tricky," Haughey was not just a random criminal or gang member. He was a politician, and he was not just any politician. From December 1979 to February 1992, he served three terms as the Prime Minister of Ireland. A key figure in the country, he was never far from scandal. As his nickname implied, questions always hung over his involvement in the illicit and backhanded. A wealthy man at a time when politicians were not that well-paid, many people struggled to comprehend where Haughey got his money. The man lived in a large house, owned a yacht and a private island, and had more than a passing interest in racehorses. Indeed, he and Stan Cosgrove even co-owned a share in Shergar.

Charles Haughey in 1967

The story that Hyde told from his prison cell involved Charles Haughey to a degree never before suggested. Though many of the plot elements were in line with what was known, there were enough revelations to make the gangster's version of events front page news. One of the chief thrusts of Hyde's story involved Charles Haughey and Stan Cosgrove and their share in Shergar. Unlike many other members of the owners' syndicate, Hyde said, the pair refused to take out additional insurance premiums on the racehorse. Indeed, Cosgrove's own son worked in the insurance industry – for Lloyds Bank, no less – and had been one of the key figures in setting up the insurance policy around the horse. It seemed strange that the broker's own father refused to sign up to the policy.

Nevertheless, Hyde recalled how he was visited in August 1982 by a man named John Addey. Addey was a famed PR man, a North London resident who had the ear and the backing of some incredibly high-profile clients. Hyde listened as Addey discussed a job that he needed done. The job was to be done for a friend and involved the kidnapping of a racehorse. To Hyde, it seemed like a fairly run-of-the-mill commission. Something that could be done easily and could bring in a large amount of illicit cash. A week passed before he was contacted again. This time, the name of the horse was revealed. It was to be Shergar, the world's favorite racing champion. Rather than the simple moneymaking scheme that he had envisaged, Hyde quickly realized that this would be utter chaos. All hell would break loose. This was not a simple job and not one which he should take. He did, however, know some people who might be able to help.

Hyde got in touch with Denis Minogue (mentioned earlier in this book) and described him as a "highly respected horseman." This much was true. Minogue was well-known for his acquaintance with the equestrian world and had even earned the respect of men such as Michael Stoute, Shergar's famous trainer. Minogue's specialty lay in breaking horses and then training them up. Both the police and the army regularly relied on the horses Minogue provided. After chatting with Hyde, Minogue agreed that he could supply both the horse trailer and "the muscle" needed for such an operation.

The trainer knew that a stallion such as Shergar would be difficult to handle and promised that a person well-versed in horses would travel with the team to help them out. This man was to be none other than Lennie Seward, a jockey with a dark past. Once well-respected in the community, Seward's career had nosedived when he became implicated in a number of betting scandals and doping cases.

After the arrangements were made, Hyde travelled back to London. There, he met with Addey and revealed the plan. The PR man provided £50,000 as an initial payment for the job in order to cover expenses. Back in Ireland, Denis Minogue had been putting together his team. This included Dominic "Mad Dog" McGlinchey, who had once been the chief of staff in the violent Irish National Liberation Army, and Jack Duggan, who could be relied upon in tricky situations. Between them, they could ensure there were no difficulties on the night. A month and a half before the kidnapping, the pair attacked two policemen in Cork. They took, as well as the uniforms, the weapons and the identification of the police. These would be used during the kidnapping.

On the night in question, Hyde believed that Seward led Shergar into the trailer while the other men held up the Fitzgerald family. The horse and trailer were then taken to Minogue's farm, whereupon they dyed the horse black and left it in a field with other racehorses. This was why cursory searches of farms in the region never revealed the truth. When trying to elude a police force who could hardly tell one horse from another, this dye job was more than enough cover. When the media caught wind of the story, this was added to the long list of bungles made by the local police.

Next, Hyde recalled, Cosgrove brought Sean Berry into the case. Tasked with handling the negotiations, Berry met with Duggan in a bar, wherein the former Army man was warned that he was being watched. Over the other side of the room, Mad Dog McGlinchey sat with a gun rolled up inside a newspaper. The event spooked Berry, and he withdrew his support. Next up, Robert Sangster put himself forward as a representative of the owners' syndicate. Sangster made it very clear that no ransom would be paid. Therefore, he suggested, the kidnappers should just leave Shergar somewhere safe so that he could be returned to the stable. Denis Minogue used his relationship with Sangster to insert himself into the middle of negotiations. Asking the owners to let him negotiate on their behalf, he began to talk to the kidnappers, the very team that he had helped put together. In addition, Minogue tricked Cosgrove into assembling £80,000 in cash to help win over the criminals' trust. As we know, this money vanished, along with all hope that the horse might be returned alive.

The story then jumped ahead 16 years. Hyde recalled how he met Denis Minogue in a pub in Effingham. Here, Minogue revealed a number of additional facts to the gangster. In this version of events, the ultimatum from Sangster was delivered to the kidnappers. When McGlinchey learned that no ransom would be paid, he took out his gun and shot Shergar in a fit of anger. McGlinchey then butchered the horse, cut it into pieces, and fed him to the pigs. The kidnappers fled the property shortly before the police arrived to perform a search in which they discovered a number of police uniforms. Minogue, who owned the farm, was given a prison sentence of four months, but his involvement in the kidnapping was not well-known. Months later,

McGlinchey got himself injured in a shootout with the police. For his many crimes, he initially faced a life sentence. But a lack of evidence brought this crashing down to 18 months. Less than a year later, Mad Dog managed to get himself caught in a firearms offence and received ten years behind bars. When he did get out, he was found shot in a phone booth in Drogheda. No one was ever arrested for the 14 bullet wounds that killed Mad Dog McGlinchey. According to legend, Duggan staged his own death and escaped to America under a different name. The rest of the gang escaped without reprisal.

John Hyde's version of the story closed with the call for an investigation into the "financial irregularities" of the owners' syndicate. Though he didn't come out and say it, he positioned men such as Tricky Charles Haughey and Stan Cosgrove as being fully implicated in the insurance scandal that followed. Rather than being an IRA fundraising effort, the kidnapping was organized and arranged by part owners in the horse. As everything escalated, short tempers and poor planning meant that Shergar was killed. The story certainly tallies neatly with many other reports. Rather than acting under the banner of the IRA, the men involved were moving in the same social circles. This could have explained why so many were quick to believe the IRA's involvement, while the word of mouth storytelling would transform mobsters into Provos in no time at all. It also helped explain bungled police attempts, the eventual fate of the horse, and just how far-reaching the conspiracy reached. That is to say, as theories go, it certainly seemed to carry some weight.

However, given the quarter of a century that passed between the kidnapping and the Hyde revelations, it seemed as though the IRA's involvement had become an accepted part of the entire affair. The case was still regarded as unsolved. Officially, there was no solution. That left the court of public opinion. After examining the evidence, each person came to their own conclusion. If, as Hyde suggested, he was the last living person with knowledge of the affair, then options with regards to knowing the entire truth could soon be gone. However, if the conspiracy went further up the ladder than previously thought (including owners and politicians, as well as British Intelligence), then there could be a huge revelation waiting to come to light. Until then, the Shergar kidnapping continues to be anybody's guess.

Conclusion

It's safe to say that no one benefitted from the kidnapping of Shergar. The racing world lost one of its brightest stars, while everyone at the stables – the grooms, the jockeys, and the owners – lost a beloved animal and friend. The Irish public lost a brief flash of positivity at a difficult time. Shergar, of course, lost his life. There was nothing gained from the entire experience on any side. Overall, there was a deep sense of shame in Ireland that one of their own might even have been behind the awful crime, regardless of personal politics or profit.

The kidnapping left a big legacy. Perhaps the first thing to change was the security surrounding stables and stud facilities. After Shergar's kidnapping, there was a sudden realization that these animals were worth major amounts of money and were essentially unguarded. There was a sudden rush to install better security features at farms around the country, something which continues to this day.

For those who had an ownership stake in the horse, what followed was a protracted legal battle. Each of the shareholders had a different insurance policy. While some were guarded against theft, some were only protected against death. With the investigators unable to prove the death of the animal but rather only the theft, that meant that some people stood to lose a huge amount of money. Among these was Stan Cosgrove, who launched a legal battle against his insurers in an attempt to reclaim his money. Joining him were a number of other shareholders, all of whom were unsuccessful.

But what of Ireland's esteemed racing industry? At the time of the kidnapping, as many as 25,000 people were employed in variously related industries. Vets, jockeys, stable boys, and everyone else were suddenly worried about the effect this might have on their livelihood. If rich backers such as the Aga Khan pulled out, then a great many people stood to lose their jobs. Luckily, the industry endured. Even today, Ireland's horseracing is a world renowned part of the sport.

In all, there was immense regret over the loss. People like Jim Fitzgerald and Walter Swinburn all came out and admitted their sadness at the disappearance of a "grand horse." In 1999, the horseracing world introduced the Shergar Cup in the horse's honor. It's been held at Goodwood and Ascot, with a unique competition format. It's regarded as a highlight of the racing calendar, a light-hearted moment when the racing community mourns the loss of a legend and proclaims their love for the sport. Even years after Shergar's kidnapping, he is having a profound effect on the sport.

Further Reading

Baerlein, R. (1984). *Shergar*. London: Joseph.

David, R. (1986). *The Shergar mystery*. Bridport, Dorset, England: Trainers Record.

Donegan, L. (2009). *Shergar - The Final Word*. HarperSport.

Halstead, S. (2015). *Shergar The IRA Backstory*. Crystal Dreams Press.

Howard, P. (2004). *Hostage*. Dublin: O'Brien.

Naden, G. and Riddington, M. (n.d.). *Burrough Hill Lad*.

Oakley, R. (2012). *The top 100 racehorses of all time*. Thriplow: Corinthian.

O'Callaghan, S. (1999). *The informer*. London: Corgi.

Sharpe, G. (2009). *Racing's greatest characters*. London: JR Books.

Thompson, D. (2013). *Too busy to die*. [Place of publication not identified]: Racing Post.

Turner, C. (1985). *In Search of Shergar*.

White, J. (2016). *Horse racing miscellany*. [Place of publication not identified]: Carlton Books Ltd.

Image Credits

1. Looking east across the broad plains of South Kildare to the distant Wicklow Hills, countryside in Ireland - self made by Sarah777
2. The Shankill road, Belfast during the troubles. From family album in my possession. circa 1970 – Fribbler
3. An IRA's ASU (Active Service Unit) displaying a Mark-10 mortar in a propaganda video (1992) – taken from video.
4. Aga Khan IV receiving a gift of Trinitite while visiting the Los Alamos National Laboratory - Los Alamos National Laboratory - Los Alamos National Laboratory
5. The racing colors of the Aga Khan. Released into the public domain by creator.
6. Charles Haughey. 22 June 1967 – Joost Evers.
7. Cover: photography of print Shergar and Walter Swinburn by Roy Miller (1981)

Excerpt from Conrad Bauer's book Tunguska: An Apocalyptic Event Beyond Belief

There was a huge explosion on the 30th June, 1908. Flattening 2,000 square kilometers of Siberian forest, the exact cause of the incredible blast is still unknown. Some have suggested that the event was caused by a meteor slamming into the Earth's surface. But no impact crater has ever been found. Other people have suggested that the meteor imploded in the sky above the forest. To this day, it is still the largest recorded impact event to strike the Earth. To this day, the explosion is still something of a mystery.

Thousands of scientific papers have attempted to get to the bottom of exactly what happened that day. With a force comparable to a nuclear blast, the destructive nature of the event is astounding. On the day, 80 million trees were knocked down, and the sound was heard across the continent. In the days afterwards, the night skies were lit up with odd lights. It was just the start of the strange series of events that would add a paranormal, perhaps even extraterrestrial dimension to the cataclysmic event.

Explosions such as these have the power to end all life on the planet. There's little that can be done when giant meteors rain down from above. The Tunguska Event not only demonstrates just how powerful such events can be, but also shows us what might happen if we survive.

Aside from the existential threat, the fallout from the blast has left a lasting impact not just on mainstream science, but on those who dig below the surface. In this book, we will examine the explosion itself and the aftereffects that have defied explanation. Trying to figure out what caused the Tunguska Event is one thing; trying to figure out how this explosion affected us as a planet is another matter entirely.

A Big Bang

The time was 7:14 in the morning on the 30th of June, 1908. This part of Central Siberia was deserted and free from almost all human life. Not many people wandered this far out into the wilderness, and it was a good thing they didn't. Right beside the bogs and swamps that lined the Stony Tunguska River, the world was about to change. While there might not have been a single person for miles around, the forests themselves were full of noise. Reindeer shuffled and strode through the woods, while birds sang and chirped in the treetops. The sun was out, a rare window of light for the dense Siberian territory. When the summer hit along the riverside, the mosquitos grew to ridiculous sizes. Hunting in swarms, they were dubbed flying alligators by those who would sometimes find themselves in this desolated part of the world.

The scene was almost idyllic. A perfect snapshot of the summer in Eastern Russia. And then it was gone. The sky was on fire, a blinding flash of the brightest light imaginable. A tower of fire swept through the heavens, measuring as high as an office block, hurtling towards Earth. Travelling roughly from the southeast to the northwest, the fire was bright enough as to leave a thick, burning trail in its wake, a shard of light nearly 500 miles long. It crashed through the sky at an incredible speed. Moving from the edge of human perception, it took just a few minutes for the giant, burning object to reach the ground.

But even before it hit, the world was drowned in an apocalyptic explosion. Lasting just over a second, the bang was bigger than a thousand atomic bombs. In some forty years' time, the Americans would drop an atomic bomb on the city of Hiroshima. This explosion was 1,000 times the size.

Almost instantly, over 2,000 square kilometers of the forest were flattened. The area along the banks of the Tunguska River would never be the same again. The animals were killed instantly, the birds caught with a song in their throats. The trees lay stripped and bare on the ground, seeming as though they had been felled and prepared as telegraph poles. Taking a wider view, the massive number of destroyed trees might look like someone had dropped a thousand boxes of matches all at once. Just as the silence started to return to the world, a thick mushroom of dirt and dust swelled up into the sky. It could be seen from incredible distances, the tower of smoke reaching almost eighty kilometers high. As quickly as all of the dirt, earth, and dust had been swept up, it began to rain down on the Earth once again. The crunching rainfall of the debris was the only sound to be heard in this stretch of Siberia.

This huge explosion took its name from the River at the epicenter of the destruction. The Tunguska Event, as it became known, is the single largest explosion in recorded human history. It beggars belief when attempting to comprehend the sheer scale of the damage and the strength of the blast. The event has become an obsession for some, who have tried desperately to explain how something just this destructive could ever happen and whether, importantly, it could ever happen again. For years, scientists have provided competing explanations for what happened that day. None have been able to comprehensively describe the exact events.

There are a huge number of questions that foil every scientist's attempt to explain the Tunguska Event. One of the best examples of this is the fact that no crater, crash site, or landing area has ever been found. Another is what happened to the trees, which were stripped and scattered rather than being uprooted and incinerated. No fragments of meteorites have been discovered. No eye witnesses were anywhere close to the area most affected.

Among the ideas put forward have been black holes, anti-matter, ball lightning, mirror matter, and secret government programs. But none have reached an entirely satisfying conclusion. While the most commonly accepted idea includes a giant asteroid crashing into the Earth, even this theory has its flaws. Even the aftermath of the event has allegedly left a strange influence on the area, one that is never normally discussed. During the course of this book, we will attempt to find a satisfying, scientific means of explaining the events of that fateful June morning.

Back in Tunguska on the morning on the event, the blast was starting to attract attention. Vanavara, a trading station, is located some 70 kilometers away from the affected area. A man named S. B. Semenov who lived in Vanavara remembered how he had been sitting on a chair outside his home when the force of the explosion knocked him to the ground. The air had grown so hot that his shirt almost seemed to be on fire. As he recalled, there was just a moment when he could see a "bright blue tube" lighting up the sky over an enormous area, after which everything fell dark. He lost consciousness shortly after, but he awoke moments later to find that the entire house was shaking to the point of collapse. The foundations were rumbling, and the walls shuddering. Windows were shattered, and a nearby barn collapsed. The air was still unfathomably heated, and the wind was rushing through the area, carrying dust and debris past the homes and down the streets, radiating out from the source of the explosion.

Elsewhere in Vanavara, a man named P. P. Kosolopov was walking outside his house. When the blast struck, he clapped his hands over his burning ears and tried to run back inside the building. Pieces of the ceiling were falling down and the stove blew out. The glass in his windows also shattered, while a sound like thunder echoed in the north. As soon as he could, Kosolopov stepped into the street to find everything settled after the clamor and chaos of the shockwaves.

Even to the north of Vanavara, people were affected. A small nomadic community had set up their tents in the hills, only for them to be snatched up into the air by the force of the blast. The people were left covered in bruises and confused by what had happened. One of their number, an old man, broke his arm. He had been picked up and thrown against the trunk of a tree. To another elderly member of the group, the event had been so shocking as to induce a heart attack.

The trees outside of the main site were perhaps even more affected than those close by. The event did enough to start a number of fires, which began along stretches of the treelines many miles away. These sparks grew into raging fires, and great herds of reindeer were caught in the infernos. The whole wildfire brought a thick cloud of smoke that billowed through the forest and prevented anyone from getting too close to the site.

The Tunguska River was hugely affected. Those who were fishing on boats and preparing their vessels were hit by both the blast and a rolling wave that threw them from their boats and into the air. On the banks, their horses panicked and stumbled as they tried to break free of their tethering. A further 200 kilometers away, a farmer was plowing his fields on a hillside. His horse dropped to its knees when it heard the sound of the explosion. Remembering it sounding like gunfire, the farmer could see the trees nearby bending in half. The soil he was trying to plough was blown up around him, while he could see a huge wave racing down a nearby river. Looking to the south, he could see the pillar of fire rising up into the sky.

The force of the impact was felt hundreds of kilometers away. We can gather as much as possible about those who were near the site, but some of the more telling stories were from those who were barely in the same country. For example, the Trans-Siberian Express is the famous train that runs across Russia. As it travelled some 600 kilometers away, the carriages were shaking on the tracks, jarring passengers wildly around in their cabins. According to the driver, the tracks ahead were rippling, and so he slammed on the breaks, just in time for the thunderous sounds to reach him. Even at 700 kilometers away, people in Znamenskoye could see the bright lights rising up into the air. The sounds were audible to people in Achayevskoye, some 1,200 kilometers away, who reported hearing sounds like gunfire sounding out in the morning and lasting for a number of minutes.

But the extreme reach of the Tunguska Event was not only limited to Russia. Part of the reason why is has become so famous is because of just how global an event it became. It was indeed the largest explosion in recorded human history, heard around the globe's largest country, so it should perhaps not be a surprise to trawl through newspapers from around the world and read about strange phenomena appearing to people in distant and remote corners of the planet, people who had never heard of Tunguska until that fateful morning.

At the time, St. Petersburg was as distant from Siberia as could be. Though technically both in Russia, they were at opposite ends of the country, with the city long being held as one of the cultural links to Europe, the part of the Russian Empire that bore the strongest ties to places such as France, Great Britain, Italy, and Germany. In that regard, there was a strong interest in the nascent science of geology, and a team had set up a device to measure earthquake activity in the western Russian city. This measuring station managed to pick up the Tunguska Event despite being placed almost 4,000 kilometers away. The bang was so large that even similar stations around the planet managed to take readings for the exact same event at the exact same time.

But it was not just a physical impact left by the Event. All around the world, people were beginning to notice strange aftereffects. Of particular note were the disturbances in the Earth's magnetic field. Just like when nuclear devices are detonated, the impact on the surrounding meteorology is huge. A station in Irkutsk had been set up to take meteorological and magnetic readings and recorded a magnetic storm that lasted over four hours. When scientists poured over the data gathered about the storm, they traced the root cause all the way back to Tunguska.

Over in the United States, it would take two weeks before a similar facility in Washington D.C. recorded similarly strange happenings. The Smithsonian Astrophysical Observatory, as well as the Mount Wilson

Observatory, took detailed notes of the strange decrease in the transparency of the air. Subsequent analysis has pointed towards the pillar of fire in Tunguska for causing the loss of several million tons of material burned up in the atmosphere by the singular event. In just a moment, the fireball had achieved something that it normally takes a year's worth of meteorites falling on the Earth to achieve.

As a result, there were marked changes to the skies on the nights that followed. On the evening of the Tunguska Event, people in Spain were able to gaze in awe at the bright and colorful patterns that were etched out on the dusk sky. The Astronomical Observatory in Heidelberg attempted to photograph this event, but the sheer brightness of the sky ruined their pictures. One photographer in Hamburg stepped out at 11pm to take a photograph of what he considered to be volcanic dust (recollections of the immediate aftermath of the explosion of the Krakatoa volcano in his mind). Meanwhile, those in Antwerp reported their surprise to see the skyline supposedly "on fire." Such reports were backed up by a newspaper published in Stockholm, in which these "strange illuminations" were perplexing the residents of the city.

One of the newspapers most interested in the Tunguska Events and its aftermath was the Times of London. They published a letter a few days after the event, for example, in which a reader described the "strange light" she had seen in the sky on the 1st of July, the day after the explosion. The writer, Miss Katherine Stephen, requested that someone explain the strange phenomena she had seen. The next day in the same paper, a man named Holcombe Ingleby attempted to provide a similarly perplexing observation, suggesting he had recently seen "curious sun effects." Despite the confusion as to the origin of the weird lights, they were revered as being of exquisite beauty.

At the time, news travelled slowly. Attempting to gather information about the exact happenings of the Tunguska Event in the immediate aftermath was almost impossible for a British newspaper. It is still difficult to this day, despite the technology that we now possess. The myriad claims and suggestions that appear scattered around the world's press at the time indicate the extent to which the explosion reached people, as well as the confusion it caused.

As such, it fell to the Times to attempt to supply an answer. On the 4th of July, four days after the Event itself, the newspaper admitted that similar phenomena, such as the lights in the sky, had been glimpsed across Europe. They admitted that there were many conflicting opinions about what had caused such a thing to happen. Some suggested that they were similar to the Northern Lights, the aurora borealis that is glimpsed in countries near the Arctic Circle. They also likened the events as being similar to the strange glows seen in the days following the Krakatoa eruption, admitting that there may have been an undocumented and unreported volcanic explosion elsewhere in the world. To put it simply, they did not have any idea.

In the United States, the New York Times was having an equally difficult time attempting to explain what was happening. They noted that there had been numerous reports of a yellow and white light that appeared in the sky for two nights, lasting until dawn each time. By way of an explanation, the paper suggests that "changes on the sun's surface" might be the cause of all of the strangeness. After a few days, the American paper reported claims from reporters in London and began to write about the global nature of the phenomena. As per their reports, people in London were so confused that they called the police stations and gave reports that the north of the city must be on fire.

Over the coming days, the brightness in the skies began to die down. From all over the world, from Scotland to Austria to America to Russia, reports were sent around the world as everyone attempted to figure out just what on Earth had happened. The stories were not even limited to tabloid sensationalism. Scientific journals such as Nature reported on the findings, providing data and observations to back up the strangeness but still falling short of an explanation. One of the most interesting observations came from two members of the British Association for the Advancement of Science, Mr. Shaw and Mr. Dines, who had invented an instrument known as the microbarograph. The tool was designed to measure sudden alterations in atmospheric pressure beyond what one might normally expect from a barometer. At the meeting of the Association, Mr. Shaw showed findings from six different examples of the microbarograph (each at a different location) that were taken in the hours following the Event. All of the findings showed four distinct peaks, indicating huge changes in the planet's pressure over the course of an hour. Accordingly, the scientists at the meeting put the strange findings down to a huge disturbance in the atmosphere at an as-yet-unknown location somewhere in the world.

But if the rest of the world was confused about what was happening in the night sky, then those who were much closer to the incident were not much better informed. However, the Siberian newspapers that were located much closer to the event also had more to report on. While the phenomena to reach Europe and the Americas was largely a visual one, those people who were closer to the Event knew about the full force of the explosion.

Newspapers such as Sibir in Irkutsk began to cover the story in depth. Two weeks after the Tunguska Event, they carried a story in which descriptions from villagers in Nizhne-Karelinskoye pointed towards far more than pretty lights. The stories from the people in the village indicated that there had been a huge body of white-blue light that took the form of a immense pipe. It was too bright to look at directly and began to move downwards in a vertical manner, carrying on for ten minutes before crashing into the forest. After this, a wall of black smoke began to move up and away from the crash site in every direction. The forest around was pulverized. The sound was deafening, as though large stones were falling or guns were shooting all around. Every building and home in the village began to shake. To the villagers, it seemed like the end of the world. Accordingly, they panicked.

Certain members of the Sibir's reporting team were close enough to hear the explosion themselves. One was in Kirensk, roughly 500 kilometers from the Tunguska Event. He too heard the long, drawn out sounds that echoed around the world, sounding like gunfire. He said the sounds came in bursts, a series of ten fifteen-minute periods that repeated and shattered the windows in the town's buildings.

One of the best descriptions came from the newspaper named Krasnoyarets, published in the town of Krasnoyarsk, which had a reporter stationed in Kezhma (just over 200 kilometers from the crash site.) This is the newspaper story closest to the event, the only one to come from an inhabited place that was anywhere near the explosion on the day in question. Like many of the other reports, there are descriptions of the shaking of buildings, loud noises, and general panic. However, this report not only suggests that "a subterranean shock" might be the cause, but also lists descriptions of a "heavenly body" of fire that rips through the sky from south to north. It was so big, unexpected, and quick that those who saw the body of fire could not hope to provide an exact impression. The moment that the fiery object touched the horizon, a tower of flame shot up into the air and split the sky into two. Just as soon as this vanished, then the sounds of the explosion reached the witnesses. The sound terrified the horses and cows in the village, who broke free and began to run wildly around. No one could tell where the booming sounds were originating.

This description is borne out by others from the area surrounding Tunguska. All of them seem to recall a "tongue of fire" appearing in the sky, like a beam shot through the sky and into the ground. In addition to the moment of the Event, the Siberian newspapers carried descriptions of the aftereffects. Just like the rest of the world, there were stories about the bright lights during the night and the shiny clouds that crawled across the sky. But it was difficult to collect together a definitive image of what had occurred on that day. The Russia of 1908 was vastly different from what we might have expected. Even in comparison to other Empires of the time, the Russia rulers had a number of challenges that prevented them from gathering information in the manner they might have preferred. One of our best insights into what was reported of the Tunguska Event comes the Trading Industrial Gazette, a newspaper published in St Petersburg. On the 4th of July, 1908, they placed a small article in their paper that was titled "The Fall of the Meteorite." In the article was simply the contents of a telegram the paper had received, mentioning that though the noise had been "considerable," they were not able to confirm anything else. According to the telegrammed report, "no stone fell."

About the Author

Conrad Bauer is passionate about everything paranormal, unexplained, mysterious, and terrifying. It comes from his childhood and the famous stories his grandfather used to tell the family during summer vacation camping trips. He vividly remembers his grandfather sitting around the fire with new stories to tell everyone who would gather around and listen. His favorites were about the paranormal, including ghost stories, haunted houses, strange places, and paranormal occurrences.

Bauer is an adventurous traveler who has gone to many places in search of the unexplained and paranormal. He has been researching the paranormal and what scares people for more than four decades. He also loves to dig into period of history that are still full of mysteries, being an avid reader of the mystic secret societies that have mark history and remain fascinating and legendary throughout the times. He has accumulated a solid expertise and knowledge that he now shares through his books with his readers and followers.

Conrad, now retired, lives in the countryside in Ireland with his wife and two dogs.

More Books from Conrad Bauer

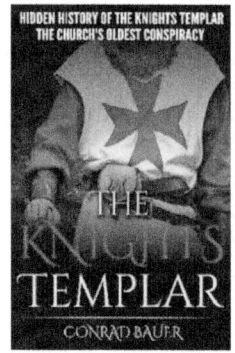  

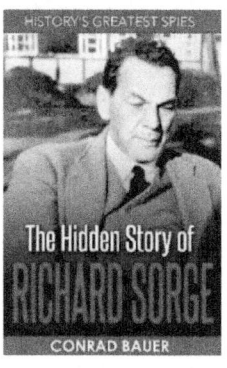  

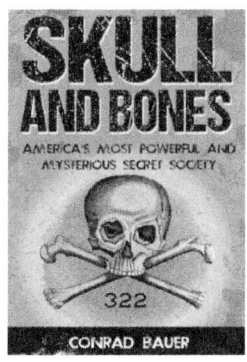

Printed in Great Britain
by Amazon

86850220R00078